Lighting Your Way, With Love

A father shares faith and wisdom with his son

Walt Lichtenberger

Copyright © 2019 Walt Lichtenberger

All rights reserved.

Cover design by Casey Fuerst, Tic Tac Toe Marketing.

All scripture quotations are from the New Revised Standard Version, Bible, copyright 1989, Division of Christians Education of the National Council of the Churches of Christ in the United States of America. Used by permission. All rights reserved.

978-0-578-42759-1

DEDICATION

To Those Who Have Lighted My Way With Love

Katie, Noah, Mark, Mom, and Dad

CONTENTS

Acknowledgments	i
Preface	iii

CHAPTER ONE

Something to Put in Our Pocket	1
What's Your Word about God?	4
Jesus Stories Are Not Just for Kids	10
A Space for Our Spirits to Grow	14
It Takes Practice	20

CHAPTER TWO

God	26
Hesed	31
The Way of a Patient Gardener	37
Beyond the God of Your Box	43
Compassion	48
Worship with Everything Ya Got!	53
A Prayer for Busy Feet	58

CHAPTER THREE

Creation	65
Bara and Ktizo	69
Co-Creating Christ	75
Beautiful, Brittle, and Brutal	81
Walking with Humility	88
To Till and Keep the Garden	94
A Walk in the Park	100

CHAPTER FOUR

Evil	106
Loving Your Enemies	111
The Storm That Made Fishermen Cry	117
When Evil Loses Its Fangs	122
Mercy and Forgiveness	127
Seeking Peace	132
Praying for Your Enemies	139

CHAPTER FIVE

Won't You Be My Neighbor?	145
Imago Dei	149
To Be or Not To Be a Neighbor?	153
You Are about To Host a *Big* Party	159
Inclusion	164
Hospitality	170

Praying with a Pen	175

CHAPTER SIX

Looking in the Mirror	180
Real Presence	184
Letting Go of Our Inner Pharisee	190
You Are Never Alone	195
Gratitude	200
Generosity	206
Breathe	211

CHAPTER SEVEN

Conclusion	218

ACKNOWLEDGMENTS

This work started as an online devotional series. I am grateful for the positive feedback that I received from my readers. It was your support that motivated me to rework and add to the material to transform it into a book. Thank you.

A debt of gratitude is also owed to my parents, who gave me life. Throughout the years, your wisdom and guidance have helped me. I am particularly grateful for your encouragement in publishing my first book. Thank you.

The ideas and concepts contained within this book come from over a quarter century of theological reflection, instruction, and public ministry. I would be remiss if I didn't acknowledge my teachers, co-learners, and friends who helped to shape, reshape, and renew my working theology. I am grateful for the faculties of Gettysburg Lutheran Theological Seminary, Philadelphia Lutheran Seminary, and Union Presbyterian Seminary, Richmond. You laid and strengthened the foundations for my public ministry giving me a language that I would use to frame and proclaim the Gospel of Jesus Christ.

To The Rev. Dr. Paul Galbreath, I share perpetual thanks. You opened Jesus's table of grace and love to me in such a way that it has forever changed my faith and ministry. To The Rev. Dr. Murdoch MacPherson, as you rest in God's peace, I am eternally grateful. You taught me how to be a pastor more than all the books that I could ever possibly read or write. To The Rev. Dick Bruesehoff, I thank you for being a companion and guide along my ongoing spiritual journey. Your regular insight continues to help me grow in my faith.

In the publishing and promotion of this book, I wish to

thank Casey Fuerst. You are a gifted designer and have been incredibly generous in helping me to tell the story of this book. I cannot say enough good things about you and your company- Tic, Tac, Toe Marketing. Thank you for a beautiful cover design.

Finally, I want to thank my family who shines the light of God into my heart. I am grateful for the daily lessons that they teach me about love, and for the forgiveness and joy which allows me to grow.

For my wife, Katie, you have forever changed me with your love. Your wisdom has challenged my biases and presuppositions while offering the comfort needed to allow me the necessary space to improve. Thank you for all your caring support for not only this book but to all my work, ministry, and life.

For my boys, Noah and Mark - it is an incredible honor to be your father. From the moment of your births, you have taught me more than it would be possible to squeeze into the pages of any book. I learn daily from you and hope that my attempt to put some of that wisdom into this book might serve as a resource for you as you navigate the transitions of your life. Thank you. I know that I won't always be able to travel down each road with you, but I will always love you both.

Though I wrote this book on the occasion of Noah starting university, and I mention him by name throughout each chapter - the book is intended to be for Mark, too. I write out of love to share my undivided love for you both. If it shines a little light on your path as you grow in your faith and identity as a child of God, then to God be the glory.

-Walt Lichtenberger

PREFACE

From the moment I wheeled the plastic hospital crib from the birthing room to get him weighed, I was smitten—completely in love with my son, Noah. In those first moments of life, he was so precious, vulnerable, and fragile. I was both amazed at the miracle of birth I had just witnessed and bewildered as to what I should do next. Though I had been preparing for months, I was suddenly a father. I was responsible, along with his mother, for taking care of and helping to shape this little person.

To this day, parenting has been a great privilege and adventure. Three years, three days, and within thirty minutes after Noah's arrival, my sense of honor and love were doubled when Mark joined our family. I am truly thankful to God for the gift of my family. Over the years together we have each grown through ups and downs, good times and bad. Change and transition seem to be constant companions on our combined journey.

This fall, Noah begins university. It has been almost two decades since I was in that hallway in Morristown Memorial Hospital, wheeling him to get weighed. He no longer fits in anything little. Matching that increased size is the expansion of the person who he has become and is in the process of developing. I am proud of my son. Of both my sons. For the purpose at hand, though, I will be focusing on Noah. It is his departure for university, after all, that has pushed me to write this book.

As he leaves to attend the University of Minnesota in Duluth, I'm taking a moment to summarize for him what has given me comfort, guidance, inspiration, motivation, and strength. As a father who is also a pastor, I'm sharing my faith.

It isn't that he hasn't heard these things before. Maybe I'm more restating them for me—to help me navigate these changing waters of life. Writing is part of my prayer life and helps me clarify the theology at the heart of my life's work of teaching and preaching the Gospel.

As a father who is also a pastor, I want to send my son to school with some useful words. These are not canned "words of wisdom" or fatherly advice. I wish I could tell him the secret to making life perfect. If only I could give him the magical incantation that would hold back the forces of evil and make every day full of rainbows and sunshine. But I can't. That isn't how life works.

What is more, to presuppose that I have all the answers to the questions with which he will struggle is a bit arrogant on my part. My challenges and struggles, after all, might not be his. Besides, even though I am in the midpoint years of my life, I am still figuring living out. I don't know it all. I remain a student of life, a work in progress.

What I can do, however, is to share some ideas that have percolated up from my experience. As a pastor, a preacher of God's good news found in the life, death, and resurrection of Jesus, I have thought about faith a bit over the years and have a few things to say on the matter. I also have a faith to share that has sustained, challenged, shaped, and comforted me in my journey through many transitions.

It is this that I endeavor to share with Noah and with you. In *Lighting Your Way, With Love*, I will share faith and words of wisdom that I hope will inspire, comfort, and strengthen. Further, I intend this book to accompany you through whatever life transition in which you may find yourself. A lil' something for the road.

CHAPTER ONE

SOMETHING TO PUT IN OUR POCKET

My father worked not as a preacher but in a tire warehouse. For long days, he rolled tires. He told me once that the mark of a good sermon was one that gave him something to put in his pocket to think about during the week. That is what I want to provide for you: something to take with you during your day. Maybe it is a word or an idea or a story that will linger long enough to be useful.

As I mentioned, I am a work in progress, a student of God's kingdom who continues to grow, learn, and be stretched by the work of the Holy Spirit. I write, pray, and live in the sure and certain hope that God is with me, forgives me, and loves me. Rooted in this sacred relationship, I share my faith with my son at the start of a significant stage in his life. It is my prayer for him (and for you) that he will lean into his own relationship with his Creator and heavenly Parent and, in so doing, find meaning, joy, and delight in this incredible adventure called life.

A NOTE TO MY SON:

Dear Noah,

When we moved you to your dorm, I was surprised that you had packed a toolbox. I know of your great love of fixing things, tools, and tinkering, but there are folks at Housing who can help should something break in your room or down the hall. Don't forget to let them know if anything needs attention.

The more I think of it, though, a toolbox is a great item to have along. You really never know what you'll need until the situation arises. Having the right tool at hand can be a godsend.

The same is true when you talk about your faith. Having a spiritual toolbox, filled with your working theology, values, ethics, dreams, and prayer practices does come in handy in life. During moments of joy and sorrow, it is useful to open your spiritual toolbox and engage your faith. It is my hope that your mother and I have given you a starter set of tools to use. You will need to add some of your own as you go along. Personally, I recommend finding a community where you can worship, pray, and belong. You might want to check out Lutheran Campus Ministry—think of it as a place where you can pick up some really cool tools.

Love you always,

Dad

A PRAYER FOR YOU:
Gracious God,
You have created us to live in community; gifted us with family; and placed us into your body, the church. At times of transition, we can find ourselves apart from the ones we love. Be with them and us. Keep us close even though time and space may separate. Remind us all of your steadfast love and care. Through Jesus Christ, amen.

What's Your Word about God?

Okay, so when you hear the word, "theology," what is your initial reaction? Are you a little intimidated? Perhaps even turned off? I remember sitting in my first theology class in seminary and feeling overwhelmed and inadequate. Theology as a course of academic study relies heavily on philosophy; I was a business major. Though I had gone to a few Bible studies and was involved in the liturgical life of my home church, I was not a theologian and seriously doubted at the time that I'd ever become one.

In academia, theology has its own language and logic. Some of it is dense stuff that requires a lot of pondering and pontificating. As I sat in that seminary classroom in Gettysburg, I recall fretting, wondering if there was a place for me in the church. How could I be a pastor if I couldn't do theology? Within a short time, though, I discovered two things that made these questions irrelevant.

First, although it seems strange initially, theology as a course of study relies on a unique language, and languages can be learned. If you crack the code, all those big three- and four-syllable words, it becomes manageable. Second, and far more critical, is that everyone already has a theology, which may or may not align with that of the ancient philosophers or prominent thinkers of the time. Put simply, theology is a "word (logos)" about "God (Theos)." We *all* have a theology because we have all thought about God. Even the most petulant atheist has a theology. Ironically, saying that there is no God is, in fact, a word about God. Even children have a theology. Ask a little one to tell you something about God and you will be surprised at the answers.

If we all have a theology, then we are all theologians of a sort. On a regular basis, consciously or unconsciously, we make adjustments and additions to our theology. Experiences in life can add positive or negative ideas about God to our "working" theology. For example, you find the love of your life. From the experience of being in love, you might say that God, who is the source of love, brought you together with your beloved. Or perhaps you just suffered the death of a loved one. Speaking from the depth of your loss, you might be angry at God and say that God doesn't care about human struggles.

At this point, you might be thinking: This is all interesting, but what is the point? Do we need a theology at all? Does it matter what my "working theology" is? How does it relate to what I'm doing now in the real world? Can't I get by without it?

Sure, you can get by in life without giving much thought to God. You can survive without a working theology, just as you can survive without exercising or eating healthfully. There are lots of things that we can avoid in life, but all our choices have consequences. Pay no attention to your body and you will find that unhealthy lifestyles take a toll. Pay no attention to God and you will experience a hurting spirit. If you don't exercise, you will find that your body may be wanting in the physical activity department. Likewise, if you don't work on your theology, you might discover that your soul is wanting spiritually.

Maintaining a working theology—*here is what I believe to be right about God*—is one component of spiritual care. Connected to it is an active worship and prayer life. These areas work together to make up our faith.

Spiritual care takes some effort on our part. Being open to God's work in our life, our response to God, and the implications that our faith has for our relationships with others is an interactive enterprise requiring our participation. It is also ongoing.

At times of transition in life, our theologies are likely to be tested in a way that previously wasn't the case. Even regular worship attendees who pray every day might find themselves coming up spiritually short. This situation is particularly real in times of loss. New questions, some of them quite disturbing, might crowd out what we previously held to be true about God. We might feel angry or hurt—like God is punishing us or doesn't care about us. Ideas and images about God, one we've long held or even treasured, may no longer seem to fit our life circumstances. What to do?

I mentioned above that the task of theology is an unfinished work. In trying times, it's back to the proverbial drawing board. Time to return to the basics and foundation of our faith. Engage in the mantra: I believe, help my unbelief. Breathe deeply. Pray with a yearning desire for that peace which passes all understanding. Seek God outside your previously constructed box. Have the courage to wade into the turbulent waters and tension of the present in the hope that the God who was seen hanging on a cross is present in life's most difficult places. Did I mention, breathe?

Throughout each chapter of *Lighting Your Way, With Love*, I will offer a theological idea for you to ponder. Some of these ideas have been mulled over throughout the centuries, while some come from more recent encounters. I share these words about God so that you can think about them and hold them up to your working theology. Do they work for you? Or do they challenge? Do they cause you to rethink and create a fracture into which a fresh perspective might creep? What is *your* word about God?

A NOTE TO MY SON:
Dear Noah,

I have watched you grow as a child of God. I was there at your baptism. You were tiny and were held by your family on that November day in 1999. Even Great-Grandma had a chance to hold you and adore you. On the day of your baptism, we celebrated your life with God. We delighted in God's promises to always be with you, no matter what.

These days, I can't hold you entirely in my arms. You're

too big. You grew! I am thankful for the person that you are becoming. I am also grateful that God's love for you continues.

It is my prayer that you will grow in your faith. I pray that you will think about God in your day. Question. Doubt. Wrestle. Work on your theology in the context of your worship and prayer life. Nurture and care for your spiritual health so that you might know delight and joy on the good days and have strength and comfort on the rough days.

Love you always,
Dad

A PRAYER FOR YOU:
Gracious God, you were present as the first molecules of air filled my infant lungs. When I take a deep breath, you fill my body with life. There is not enough praise or thanks that I can give to you, my Creator and Sustainer. Help me this day to connect my heart, head, and hands with you, giver of life. Open my being so that I might grow as your child. Through Jesus Christ, amen.

Jesus Stories Are Not Just for Kids

My grandfather played a prominent role in my life as I was growing up. I recall as a teenager spending many a Friday afternoon sitting with him on folding lawn chairs in my backyard.

Grandpa was a World War II veteran; he served in a bomb disposal unit in Europe. He didn't linger on the horror or the destruction of the war much. There was only one story that he told me in which someone died. Instead, the epic adventures focused more on friendships and how a small group of GIs survived and made their way "somewhere in Europe." Grandpa knew the power of stories to connect with others.

It has been almost twenty-four years since we laid my favorite storyteller to his eternal rest. Still, his stories continue. They live in me. I continue to treasure Grandpa's epic adventures and retell them from time to time.

Jesus knew the power of stories. It is no mistake that we read in the Bible that Jesus's teaching consisted of parables. These little stories of ordinary instances and common objects connected with his hearers, bringing with them big truths about God and God's Kingdom. Like my Grandpa, Jesus was a master storyteller who knew how to connect his narrative with the lives of his hearers.

Long after the Nazarene left to go on to the next town, the people there remembered and treasured what he said. What is more, they passed the teaching on to others until the Gospel writers (Matthew, Mark, Luke, John) eventually wrote them down. Not only did Jesus's stories make the canonical cut, but so did dozens of stories about Jesus's life and ministry.

One might view the entire Bible as a giant storybook. You could say that it is a love story of sorts between God and people, full of adventure, intrigue, suspense, brokenness, and redemption. By the time the tale gets to Bethlehem, a pattern has emerged between God and the people: God is faithful and steadfast in love, people stray and seek life apart from the source of their life. God doesn't give up but instead enters the story in real time in the presence of Jesus. People turn back to God and live.

These "Jesus" stories are valuable. Taken together, they help to hold back the curtain, giving us a glimpse of God's hidden nature, which is beyond our comprehension. By the hearing, telling, and treasuring of the stories of Jesus's life and ministry, we have an invaluable resource. Taking Jesus stories to heart, we will be inspired, instructed, and empowered in our living. They are even helpful at times when we find ourselves missing the familiar occupants of the lawn chairs in our backyard.

A NOTE TO MY SON:

Dear Noah,

What stories do you remember from when you were little? Do you recall "Moo, Baa, La La La?" I must have read that story to you a thousand times. Okay, maybe that's a slight exaggeration. Still, I read it enough to know it by heart. It is a story that kinda sticks with you.

As I'm missing you, I'm doing a lot of remembering. Storybooks. Pictures. They bring both a smile and a little sadness. Memories of the past are treasures that live in my heart. The sadness comes from being apart. But that is the way life goes—joy and tears are often companions in our journey.

I hope that you are well and that you are happy today. Remember that at the heart of Jesus's story were kindness, compassion, inclusion, and love. May you have the wisdom, courage, and faith to keep such things close at hand as you write the next chapter of your own story.

Love you always,
Dad

A PRAYER FOR YOU:
Gracious God, throughout the ages, your story is one of steadfast love and faithfulness. From creating all people in your image to your deliverance of your people from captivity, you liberate life itself. Strengthen me to live in your story this day. Guide me in your path so that my life might reflect your goodness. Through Jesus Christ, amen.

A Space for Our Spirits to Grow

It was a beautiful day. The sky was a cerulean blue with scattered, wispy clouds. I walked along the top of a prairie ridge. Grasses yielded to the gentle pressure of a refreshing wind. It was hard to take it all in. Such simplicity. Calm. In reverence, I admired the timeless artistry of nature. I wondered: *Is this what heaven is like?*

Imagination. It is an indescribable gift that helps us to see with an inner vision. When we imagine something, we look beyond the constraints and limitations of the present. New possibilities and directions can suddenly emerge as we tap into our creative selves.

At this point you might be asking: What does imagination have to do with faith? Doesn't faith deal with certainties and unwavering belief? Isn't the gift of faith God's doing in our lives; evidence that the Spirit is working in our spirits enabling us to believe? What do creativity and imagination have to do with that?

As a Lutheran pastor, I think one of the most brilliant things that Martin Luther ever wrote was his explanation of the Third Article of the Apostle's Creed: "I believe that by my own reason or strength I cannot believe in Jesus Christ, my Lord, or come to him. But the Holy Spirit has called me through the Gospel, enlightened me with his gifts, and sanctified and preserved me in true faith, just as he calls, gathers, enlightens, and sanctifies the whole Christian church on earth and preserves it in union with Jesus Christ in the one true faith."[1]

A quick read of this foundational Lutheran teaching, that our faith comes as a graceful gift and is not of our doing, might seem to say that faith is a fixed entity. What else could "true faith" be? Either we believe and have faith, or we don't. It's cut and dry. Black and white.

Though I don't doubt that you can interpret that passage in a fixed, immovable manner, I'm not sure that such an approach is, ironically, all that faithful. Let me explain. The Gospel of Jesus Christ is one of liberation, redemption, and reconciliation (how many three-syllable "holy" words can I fit into a sentence?) In short, the story of Jesus's life is about freedom, establishing a new and right relationship between a loving God and a hurting people.

---

[1] Martin Luther, "Small Catechism," translated and edited by Theodore G. Tappert in *The Book of Concord*, (Philadelphia: Fortress Press, 1959), 345.

Love becomes an expanding boundary. The Spirit moves in the direction of our hearts and opens a space for God to dwell within. Each of our spirits becomes fertile ground whence love can grow organically. This is not a one-size-fits-all proposition.

From the experience of parenting two very distinct sons, I know that my approach with each is a little different. Although I love them both with all my heart, my relationship with each reflects his individual interests, needs, and dreams. At times, it can be hard to make sure that I am even-handed and balanced. Still, it is worth it. I couldn't force a single way of relating upon my relationships with my boys. Imposing any kind of constructed "universal" parenting method would ignore their particular natures.

When the Spirit moves in our lives, it comes to each of us to work faith within our hearts that is as distinctive as our fingerprints and favorite flavor of ice cream. Sure, this is the same love of God that created the cosmos and sent Jesus to live and die among us. It is the same eternal love. And it is also profoundly personal. God connects with me and my faith in a way that is slightly different from the manner in which God relates to you.

When we exercise our spiritual imaginations, we make ourselves available to both the expansive love that God has for all creation and the unique love God has for us. We might wonder how such things can be. Where can we experience such wondrous love? What is that love calling us to do in response? These are all open-ended questions that can spark a variety of creative answers. Which are correct? Is there such a thing as a wrong answer? What if we find the solutions that we generate to be different from those of others?

As a Christian, I will always look to the life, death, and resurrection of Jesus as a guide. Do my creative faith-thoughts line up with the love of Christ? If so, then maybe I am connecting in a new way with God's Spirit. If not, then perhaps I just have a terrible case of indigestion.

I will also test the product of my imagination against the witness of scripture within the context of a broader faith community. Being creative in your faith doesn't mean anything goes. At times, we will need to check ourselves, lest we start creating God in our own image. That said, believing "outside the box" is a sign that we are engaging in our relationship with the living God in such a way that God is creating all things new.

Back to that beautiful day that I experienced on a prairie ridge. On days like that, I am filled with wonder that reaches deep within my spirit. Such days help to crack open my stagnant ideas about God, faith, and life. Space is created from the inside out to be a different person. Using our God-given imagination to cultivate the soil that finds its way into that space holds great promise for growth. In times of transition, as we seek to embrace new realities, this is indeed a gift from God.

A NOTE TO MY SON:
Dear Noah,

Do you remember how beautiful it was that day when we hiked at Blue Mounds State Park? Or maybe you remember our hike down into the little canyon at Arches National Park? Yellowstone? Grand Tetons? Vancouver Island? Our travels took us to many places, didn't they? As soon as you and your brother were big enough, we hit the trails. I know what you are thinking: death marches! Well, I suppose more than once we found ourselves in a challenging spot. But now you have the memories, so stop complaining.

I always liked hiking in nature. It gives me a chance to clear my mind and breathe deeply. More than once, I've had a slew of creative ideas after hiking. We all need that space where we can unplug, breathe, and be open to new possibilities. That space—where imagination can run wild—can be a sacred spot.

Here's hoping that you carve out some time and space to dream. Maybe head up the North Shore when you get a break from class and marching band. I'll bet there is at least one place nearby where you can go, breathe, and let your heart imagine.

Love you always,
Dad

A PRAYER FOR YOU:
Gracious God, you are beyond my grandest imagination. You exceed my wonder. Out of your expansive nature, you create and dream life into being. Although I can't begin to grasp your reality, I am humbled and honored that your love would come to me. To have you near is a joy without compare. Stir up in me, O Lord, an active imagination so that I may be open to possibilities, dream

dreams, and sing a new song of praise. Through Jesus Christ, amen.

It Takes Practice

I learned to juggle when I was in college. It took a while for me to keep three objects in the air without dropping them. I had to learn a pattern and the discipline of sticking to it. Eventually, though, as long as I could safely toss it, catch it, and it was round, I could juggle it: balls, apples, oranges, etc. I even learned a few tricks and a juggling routine, complete with comedy when I dropped something. Juggling was and continues to be a fun thing to do that entertains children of all ages, myself included.

It wasn't too long after I had mastered the basics that I decided I wanted to graduate to clubs in addition to juggling round objects. Clubs, which look like bowling pins on a diet, are the mainstay of any juggler. I already knew the criss-cross pattern of tossing and catching. Further, whenever I spun a club in the air, the extended handle portion seemed to come right back into my hand.

How hard could juggling clubs be? Famous last question.

I took a beginner set of clubs, which I'd received as a gift, into the spare bedroom of the house and closed the door. What followed wasn't pretty. I'm glad that most of what transpired remains a suppressed memory. I do recall having to spread an old sleeping bag over the furniture to protect it. It took weeks of practice in that "padded" room before I finally got it. Practice, persistence, perspiration—I needed all three.

It wasn't enough to know the theory of juggling (the toss-catch pattern) or how to spin a club so that it would land in my hand correctly. It took the hard work of actually doing it over and over before I gained any proficiency.

So it goes with the spiritual life. It is one thing to know that God loves you, accompanies you through the ups and downs of life, and wants you to live peaceably with others. It is another to practice your faith so that head, heart, and hands (the old 4-H mantra) connect in a fluid movement. Faith takes hard work.

Sadly, I've seen too many people leave their faith unpracticed. When difficulty strikes, an unpracticed faith is not all that great a resource. It is hard to turn to your spiritual core when you are not that all that familiar with it.

To be sure, working on our faith is not required for God to love us. The Bible teaches us that God's love is grace-centered and comes to us apart from our work. The unearned mercy of God, filled with forgiveness and steadfast faithfulness, remains foundational for Christians. That said, without practice, faith becomes unreal for us. There is a marked difference between owning a set of juggling clubs and being able to juggle.

As I think about navigating transitional times in life, the importance of practicing our faith comes to the forefront. How do we exercise and engage what we know and believe to be true? What daily connections might we make to the God who remains close at hand? How do we make the truth of the Gospel truth for us, so that we lean into it and take refuge within?

Back to juggling. The most basic juggling involves handling three objects in an established pattern. Of course, professional jugglers can manipulate many more balls, clubs, or rings and can even set them on fire! But let's take the simple route for starters. What three aspects of faith could we juggle on a daily basis that would serve to strengthen us spiritually?

I suggest that we focus on values, ethics, and prayer. Each of these foci interacts with a different relational sphere. Values make up personal integrity. Ethics is the application of our faith in our dealings with others and the world. Prayer is communication with God. Throughout the chapters of this devotional book, we will spend time with each. We will look at some patterns and practices. We'll struggle with some open-ended questions. The goal is to enter into intentional living based on what we hold as spiritual truth.

My son, Noah, who is very much in my heart as I write this book, knows how to juggle. A long time ago, I taught the basic "toss-catch" pattern to him and his brother. They can each do it with varying degrees of success. In addition to balls and clubs, Noah can also work the Diablo. This juggling apparatus looks like a giant yo-yo. I got one in my early years of juggling and could never quite get it to work. Noah, however, picked the Diablo up and made it his own. He can entertain you for about ten minutes with an elaborate series of interlocking skills.

Before heading out to university, he had to go to the juggling store and learn a new trick to take with him. Among all the things he packed for school were his Diablo and yo-yos (he is also proficient with them). Knowing him, he is using his free time, maybe even between classes, to develop his skills.

Practice doesn't make perfect (perfection is an unattainable fool's errand), but it does let us engage, live, grow, and thrive. It takes time, effort, and work—but it's worth it. It helps us gain confidence, strength, and familiarity. Good things to have with us whenever we try to juggle. Priceless essentials when it comes to our faith.

A NOTE TO MY SON:

Dear Noah,

How is your juggling going? Gravity might not be a juggler's friend, but practice is more than a friend—it is essential. I hope that you are taking some time out of your busy day to have some fun and throw a few things in the air. Or maybe you are working on your new yo-yo trick. Whatever you do, be sure to relax a bit.

Also be sure to take a few moments to care for your spirit. A simple prayer (silent is okay—it doesn't need to be awkward or weird) before your meals or at the start of the day. Remember that you are God's beloved child and that God wants you to love others. Tending to your spirit is like practicing a routine—the more you do it, the more it will seem like second nature. Prayer helps; so does attending worship on campus; so does living out your values and ethics. You don't need to do it all at once, just as you can't keep more than one ball in the air at a time. Amidst it all, don't forget to breathe.

Should you drop something—and you will—don't forget about that "grace" thing. God's love abounds with forgiveness! Whew!

Love you always,
Dad

A PRAYER FOR YOU:
Gracious God, be present in the midst of the busy and crazy moments of life. When everything seems topsy-turvy, unclear, and strange, remind me of your great love. Ground me in your grace. Give me the wisdom to take things one at a time. Guide me in your ways. Renew my courage to trust in you. Through Jesus Christ, amen.

CHAPTER TWO

GOD

To say that Rainier is a mountain is like saying that the Mona Lisa is a painting: accurate but woefully inadequate. When you gaze upon this stratovolcano's summit, you are in the presence of something mighty and mysterious. At 14,411 feet, this temporal titan influences weather patterns, which can change at a moment's notice and be quite severe. The picturesque view of the snow-capped peak against a blue sky belies the awesome power that lies within. Mount Rainier remains on the international "Decade Volcanoes" list, which consists of sixteen volcanoes around the world that scientists closely monitor because of their potential to erupt and proximity to large populations.

When I hiked along the trails that meander around the base of Mt. Rainier, I had a strange feeling. Somehow, even when you couldn't see the massive volcano (perhaps you were on the opposite side of a ridge, or a cloud blanket obscured it from view), the mountain was always there; you sensed its presence. Try as you might, you can't escape its charm, awe, and prominence. Rainier is a presence to be acknowledged, reckoned with, respected, and admired. As I fondly remember my experience of Rainier, humility fills my spirit. In the volcano's presence, my inflated self-importance and scattered focus seemed to dissolve. It was as though I entered a gothic cathedral at midday, when the sun shines through the large rosette window in the rear of the nave. A deep reverence overtook and slowed me down. I was left speechless and able only to breathe deep, sacred breaths.

This chapter centers on God. As we seek wisdom and light on a path through transition (for children who have left home, for parents who stay behind, and for anyone facing a significant life change), this might seem counterintuitive. Shouldn't we begin with ourselves? After all, if we are in the midst of personal upheaval, we are most likely an emotional mess. Shouldn't we be talking about personal feelings? Or, for the intellectually inclined, shouldn't we be doing some cognitive analysis?

There are many self-help and life-management books that will head in these directions. They are readily available, albeit for a pricey sum, with all sorts of outrageous claims about how they'll transform your life in five "easy" steps.

In starting with God, I seek a different kind of wisdom—the kind that exists beyond ourselves, outside our limitations, pretensions, and delusions. I yearn for grounding in things that are more lasting than the latest fad or snake oil. I want something that will genuinely nurture my spirit, not just fill it up with empty calories. In transition, I need to trust in things unseen and unknown in a materialistic and consumptive culture. I yearn for a connection to the Living God that surpasses all my understanding and construction.

More than once, on the hiking trails of Mt. Rainier, I stopped to catch my breath. Beyond the practical need to rest, which the difficulty of the path itself dictated, I had a spiritual need to pause. The massive, ever-present mountain compelled me to awe. Quickly, the majesty and mystery humbled me. A prevailing sense of peace displaced any feelings of inadequacy or insignificance. Gazing on the behemoth before me, I couldn't resist praising and worshiping the God who formed such wonders. How great Thou art! Near the mountain, my spirit was lifted and free.

Throughout this chapter, we will center on the One who is mightier than the most majestic of mountains and as close as our next breath. We will pay close attention to some aspects of God's nature that scripture reveals. I will invite you to look at your image of God and then wonder about the God who lies beyond your imagination and domestication. From an expanding perspective on God, I will also suggest we focus our energies on God's graceful nature to aid with our daily interactions with others. During times of transition and change, core values and ethics are invaluable in helping us navigate unknown territory. They are essential tools for us to use in our dealings with others. Last, I will offer you a creative way of praying that involves your shoes!

It will be a busy journey. Maybe it would be a good thing for us to stop and take a deep breath.

A NOTE TO MY SON:
Dear Noah,

Remember when we hiked in Mt. Rainier National Park? The scenery was awesome. You and your brother had to wait for your parental units to catch up (thanks, by the way). Do you recall when we stopped at an overlook for a water and picture break? I know—we did that a lot, didn't we? I'm thinking of the stop where we met the chipmunk. We sat on the stone wall and the little critter came to visit us. He was a con artist well versed in the art of mooching food from tourists. Cute and conniving. If you recall, we resisted his Jedi mind powers and chased him on his way.

As I think about that rodent, I wonder: Did it know that it lived in one of the most beautiful places we have ever visited? Did it ever take time from scurrying for bits of granola bars and Cheetos to look at the mighty mountain? Was survival its only purpose? Did it have the capacity or wisdom to stop, breathe, and give thanks to the Creator of the mountains on which it lived?

I know you are probably busy these days, rushing back and forth across the campus. Granola bars and Cheetos might even be a regular part of your diet (though don't forget the healthy choice of the salad bar in the cafeteria). Be sure to take some time. Stop. Breathe. Look up and wonder. The Creator of mountains and chipmunks loves you to the core of your being. And so do I!

Love you always,
Dad

A PRAYER FOR YOU:

Gracious God, you formed the mountains from the chaos of the deep. With power beyond my wildest imagination, you shaped and created a place where life abounds. Give me the wisdom this day to stop along my quick way. Open my senses to acknowledge your presence. Then, with awe and reverence, let me breathe fully. Through Jesus Christ, amen. Through Jesus Christ, amen.

Hesed

It didn't take a skilled pastoral listener to perceive the agony and anguish in his soul. Although it was almost twenty-five years ago, I can clearly see the nervous wringing of his hands as he sat before me. How could I forget? It was a few months into my pastoral internship in Utica, New York. "Wet behind the ears" doesn't fully capture my inexperience, both in matters of life and spirit; I was twenty-four years old and had only five semesters of seminary training. I had no prior—or subsequent—contact with the middle-aged man who sat opposite me on a folding chair in my closet-sized office, but he left an indelible impression.

He was in full spiritual crisis. Despite his multiple efforts at denial and restraint, he couldn't escape his secret identity. The Christian community where he worshipped, where he felt loved and had close friends, labeled homosexuality as an abomination, a sin above all sins, a cause of shame, and grounds for immediate dismissal. What was he to do? If only they knew, his friends would undoubtedly shun him.

To make matters worse, I found out through gentle questioning that in his heart he agreed with the judgment of his church. Based on his rigid interpretation of a few verses of an ancient holiness code (which, by the way, also abolished the eating of shrimp), God damned his sexual orientation to eternal punishment. So fixed on God's wrath and sternness was this tormented soul's working theology that grace, forgiveness, and love were unavailable to him.

As I sat across from him, my working theology wasn't much better. It would be years before I would uncover a critical aspect of God's nature—the theological concept of *hesed*—and place it at the heart of my pastoral care and the center of my life of faith.

Hesed is a Hebrew word that appears 248 times in the Bible that Jesus read. You can translate it in a variety of ways, including great mercy, kindness, loving kindness, and even goodness. It bears a sense of eager and ardent desire or zeal. *Hesed* is used to describe the relationships between people. It can also define the connection between God and people. *Hesed* is mutually beneficial and filled with grace or favor.

Time and again we read in scripture (especially in the book of Psalms) that *hesed* is part of God's nature. God is full of mercy, goodness, grace, and loving kindness. *Hesed* is how God relates to us and all of God's broken creation. What is more, God's *hesed* is a passionate endeavor. God keeps at it, despite the unfaithfulness and lack of *hesed* on the part of humanity.

We find numerous examples of *hesed* illustrated in the life, death, and resurrection of Jesus. Jesus is all about compassion, grace, generosity, acceptance, and hospitality. All these attributes emerge from and are supported by Jesus's application of *hesed*.

When you put *hesed* at the center of your working theology, something incredible happens. It causes the brimstone and frightening ideas about God to fade. In their place emerges a compassionate God who is madly in love with creation. "The LORD is gracious and merciful, slow to anger and abounding in steadfast love

(Psalm 145:8)." God is full of *hesed*, not anger, judgment, or hatred.

Further, God is *not* out to get us, waiting for us to slip up or fail. Instead, God is ever-present to support, guide, comfort, and love us. Our proper response is not anxious fear but grateful adoration.

When *hesed* defines God's identity in your working theology, you gain the freedom to love without needing to worry about whether you are getting it right. You are free to be the person God created you to be, without trying to contort yourself into a box that deforms, limits, shames, and disregards. It is *not* a license to do whatever you want. Rather, it is an invitation to engage in acts of loving kindness and mercy of your own.

Perhaps the most profound examples of *hesed* that I've seen have come from family members who care for a dying loved one. Their *hesed* humbles me as they go above and beyond, tending to not only the emotional but also the physical needs of their parent or spouse.

In my home, I watched my wife, Katie, care for her mom, Judi, in her last days. As Judi's body lost function, Katie's became stronger in her care. Although it certainly took a toll on Katie, she managed to carry on through the ordeal with grace and compassion. Judi received this gift and was able to rest knowing that she was deeply loved. That is how *hesed* works.

That is also why *hesed* deserves a place at the heart of your and my thinking about God. When we allow *hesed* to displace thoughts of wrath and judgment, a new space of possibilities opens in our spirit. God's steadfast love, mercy, goodness, and loving kindness push fear, despair, insecurity, and anxiety to the side. This movement, and the space it creates, comes as the graceful acts of a Spirit that walks with us down paths as yet untrodden, through perils and possibilities unknown.

A NOTE TO MY SON:

Dear Noah,

How's your hesed *doing today? I know that you are probably rolling your eyes at this moment. Stop. I'm serious. How are your compassion, grace, kindness, and mercy holding up?*

Pretty soon, you will be taking your first round of exams. There is judgment whenever tests enter the picture. You study. You try your hardest. And you get graded. Depending on the grade, it can be either a triumphant or defeating experience. You will soar or feel like you have crashed.

Back to hesed—*God's unlimited mercy, grace, love, and goodness for you. Nurture this truth in your heart so that no matter what the test result may be, you know that you remain a priceless Child of God. Hesed will help lift you up on those bad days and give you the courage to carry on. Hesed will also keep you humble when you ace things and make you available to those who need your help. Thus, whether you are up or down, you remain kind, compassionate, slow to anger, and abounding in steadfast love—just like your God.*

Love you always,
Dad

A PRAYER FOR YOU:

Gracious God, you abound in steadfast love. Your mercy is more abundant than my biggest failure. You love me even when I'm not so lovable. You remain with me even when I don't want to be with myself. Give me the wisdom and strength to rest in your *hesed*. Empower me in my weakness to emulate your kindness and compassion in all my living so that I may walk in your ways. Through Jesus Christ, amen.

The Way of a Patient Gardener

Jesus tells a parable about an unfruitful tree (Luke 13:6-9.) The story goes like this: The owner of a vineyard plants a fig tree. For three years, each time he checks the tree, he encounters the same result—no figs! In his anger and frustration, he calls the gardener and demands that he cut down the tree. The gardener asks for the chance to further nurture the tree, and for more time. If after a year it still doesn't produce, the gardener reasons, then he'll cut it down. Of course, we never find out what happens to the fig tree.

In classic parable style, we are left to wonder: Did the tree finally produce fruit? Did the gardener use his ax? Or did he go another round begging the owner to be patient? We will only know the answer if we continue the story in our imagination.

How patient are we with the unproductive fig trees in our own lives? Do we demand results or else? Do we follow our culture's impatience and quickly move on when something no longer suits our needs, taps our emotions, or increases our bank account?

How big is your discard pile? Were you to root through the things that you have chopped down and cut off, what would you find? Relationships. Dreams. Diets. Interests. God? Would your pile bear witness to patient restraint or insatiable consumption?

The size of our pile, its contents, and the rate at which we contribute to it all reveal something about our spiritual nature. Are we patient? Do we tolerate imperfection and work toward long-term growth? Or are we dismissive? Do we demand instant gratification?

Beyond such self-focused questions are those that point to our understanding of God. Is God patient? Does God tolerate our imperfection and lack of growth? Or is God ready to cut down, discard, and move elsewhere? Do we imagine God to be the impatient vineyard owner or the hopeful gardener?

Jesus tells this story in the context of his overall teaching about God's expansive love. God's heart, according to Jesus, beats fervently in the direction of a broken and hurting world. God seeks restoration and renewal of all life not by demanding it, but rather by inviting it. Instead of forcing change, Jesus encourages repentance (a turning toward God) and faith (a trusting in God) as a path toward abundance, joy, and life. The steadfast nature of both God's character and Jesus's approach is infinitely patient, long-suffering, and expectant.

From this perspective, I wonder if God isn't the ultimate and most hopeful of gardeners. Even though we don't produce any expected fruits, God refuses to employ an ax. In place of chopping, God gets down and works the dirt, adding additional fertilizer. Where there is life, there is still hope for growth and change. God does not assess worth on the basis of production but rather on the relationship that God established with all creation. In short, God remains faithful to us no matter what.

God will keep on being patient and looking forward to future fruit.

What might it mean for us to think of God as a patient and expectant gardener? It certainly challenges the image of God as an angry, heavenly judge that is heartlessly waiting for us to mess up. Many people retain some version of this in their working theology, and it generates unhealthy, paralyzing guilt. Negative understandings of God fuel fear and, in the long term, cause us to turn away. To know, in our spirit, that God loves us and desires our growth is liberating. Love pushes fear and guilt to the sidelines, allowing each of us the freedom to become the person God created us to be in the first place.

It might also make us pause as we reach for our axes. Instead of cutting others to the quick, we can choose a different path. Like the God who created us, we can decide to be patient. Breathing in the grace of God, we can divert from our anger-laden responses that destroy relationships and future interactions. As we exercise restraint, we are moving in the direction of repentance. It is a conscious turn toward God and away from our base instincts. Although it may seem like more trouble for us in the short run, traveling in the path of Jesus always leads to life.

A NOTE TO MY SON:
Dear Noah,

It was a couple of years ago, but do you remember helping me cut down that big dead tree in the backyard? It took us a whole day with pulleys, wedges, ropes, and a chainsaw to drop that tree. We even included Grandpa in the effort. He watched to make sure no one went near the severed but still standing tree as we headed off to FleetFarm for more supplies. When that tree finally crashed to the earth, we were exhausted and had used up all the available daylight.

At first glance, it might seem like cutting something down is the quick and easy route to solving a problem. When relationships become messy, it might look like ending them is best. When doubts make up the most significant portion of our faith, it might appear that abandoning belief makes the most sense. We live in a culture that is always ready to reach for the chainsaw. Timber! Move on!

Let me suggest a different approach, one that might be harder at first but will ultimately pay higher dividends.

Stop. Breathe. Remember that God is ever patient with you. God's way is not the way of destruction but of life. It doesn't mean that you will never have to break a relationship or let go of a dearly held belief. At one point or another, we all need to say goodbye. But let that not be your first move.

Instead of cutting down, try to nurture. Be patient and humble. Breathe. Open yourself to whatever God is up to in the situation. What lessons can you learn? How might this be an opportunity for you to grow? Linger for a moment in the tension, unease, and brokenness. Recall that this is the place of the cross. It is also the place of resurrection, new life, and hope.

Love you always,
Dad

A PRAYER FOR YOU:

Gracious God, you continue to love a wayward creation obsessed with immediate results. Your patience with us, with me, is pure grace. Let me both dwell in this gift and let it slow me down as I respond to others. Fashion in me a patient spirit that seeks to nurture rather than destroy. Guide me to live in alignment with your constant love. Through Jesus Christ, amen.

Beyond the God of Your Box

So, how big is your God?

It might seem like a silly question. Indeed, God is vast, grander than the cosmos: eternal and all. God doesn't fit in a box. Anybody knows that, or at least anybody who believes in God.

Try this follow up question: Is there anything God can't do or won't do? If I could pursue this line of inquiry with you for long enough, I'm guessing we'd eventually bump into a boundary or limitation. Each of us has, consciously or otherwise, drawn some sort of line in the sand that we can't imagine God crossing. God loves everyone *but* _____ (fill in the blank).

Using the building materials of our understanding of scripture, tradition, our family of origin, or life itself, we have each constructed a box in which we house our image of God.

From my experience in talking with a lot of people about their faith, our image of God is as big as the box that we've constructed to preserve, protect, and house our holy thoughts. It is also my experience that whenever we attempt to squeeze God into a confined space, we run into problems.

There is a temptation to go to war with others whose God boxes are different. There is also a tendency to domesticate God into irrelevance—converting the divine into a trinket that looks nice on a shelf but doesn't make much of a difference in the way we live. Either way, Jesus was never meant to be in a coffin. Neither was the Creator of the heavens, earth, and the cosmos.

A critical step on the road to a healthy spiritual life involves acknowledging that we can't escape our predisposition to box in God. Further, all boxing attempts border on blasphemy. Whenever we construct walls around God, no matter how pious or authorized our intentions, we are trying to create God in our image. It moves in the direction of playing God, and it is a sure recipe for disaster.

Our boxes—whether they are gold or cardboard—can never take the place of God. Idols will always fall short, no matter how well we have constructed them. In the face of our biggest challenges, we may discover a disconcerting truth: boxed gods are silent and powerless. *Stop.* Repent. Turn away from the box.

Here is where our spiritual imagination can play a helpful role. Imagine the God that freely lives beyond conventions, restrictions, traditions, limitations, or boundaries. Dream. Envision. What if we were to tear down one of the walls of our boxes? What new perspectives would we gain about God?

Turning our imaginations loose might seem way too chaotic for most folks. This may especially be the case for those who are in a time of transition in life. Why would we want to encourage more unease and mess? Wouldn't it be better to turn to our more familiar images of God, like the ones we grew up with on the walls of our childhood Sunday school classrooms? Shouldn't we return to the tried and true treasures of the past?

When we are in need of the living God, nostalgia offers but a small comfort. Sentimentality is no better. Past images might be quaint, but they can be a source of further confinement.

Gaining a historical perspective can help us in our imaginative quest for God, but it cannot be the goal or purpose of that search. Merely going back to our god of yesteryear will leave us ill-equipped for the challenges facing us in an ever-changing present. Instead of dusting off old containers, a better choice is to find the courage to open our boxes.

When we seek God beyond fixed images and small boxes, we allow our spirit to open at its widest point. In that place where we find ourselves unable to speak, or even think, we can only trust. Faith alone navigates these waters with a childlike acceptance. I may not get remotely close to the expansive, hidden essence of the Divine Presence. But that is okay. I don't need to unravel all mysteries. God is with me and knows my being to the very core. God's spirit is as close as my next breath. Nothing can separate or box me out. There are no limitations to God's love. No boxes.

A NOTE TO MY SON:
Dear Noah,

I know that you have a box or two in your dorm room from when we moved you there. That was an emotional day for me, for you, and for our whole family. Into boxes, you packed essentials: clothes, snacks, tea kettle, etc. You also put a few of your favorite things: a Star Wars *action figure, a LEGO sculpture, your pillow, and so on. Your room contains these things now, and I hope that they are making the dorm space into a home away from home—a place of rest and comfort where you can be yourself. The boxes, now empty, are on the shelf awaiting your next move.*

Boxes are useful things, don't you think? You can use them to cart, store, and protect treasures and everyday things. They are good for helping us to manage our stuff.

But boxes are less useful when they serve as the metaphoric containers for our ideas about God. When we box up nice, neat, unchangeable ideas about God, they can be a detriment to our faith. They are restrictions that we place on God's ability to create, love, reform, and act. It is a crazy thought that we can even do this—who are we to tell God what to do? Still, it is a thought that comes to our minds as we seek to make sense of a crazy world.

Best if we left the boxes for our stuff. When it comes to God, we should be open-minded.

Love you always,
Dad

A PRAYER FOR YOU:

Gracious God, create in me an active imagination that remains open to your presence, which remains beyond my attempts to control and contain. Through Jesus Christ, amen.

Compassion

Living in Minnesota, I have learned that ice is a formidable foe. During my first winter in this northern clime, I made the rookie mistake of leaving a case of soda pop in the trunk of my car overnight. In the morning, the back of my vehicle looked like a crime scene. There was sticky, slushy residue everywhere, littered with empty, distorted cans. What a mess!

At times, our environment can be unforgiving and downright harsh. Transitions can be especially tricky. Familiar comforts or people may no longer be available to help us through our challenges. It might feel as though we are suddenly alone and without a clear idea of what we should do next. It is here that our values come into play and can play a guiding role.

Values are the principles by which we live. They guide, inspire, and direct us because they are the things that we hold most dear. We aspire to live in this way because we know that it leads to something more significant. Everyone has a set of values—even scoundrels and villains. Experience, faith, family, and culture all participate, over time, in shaping our values. Wisdom remembers and applies these principles to a variety of situations. Paradoxically, values need to be flexible enough to fit changing circumstances, yet fixed enough to offer clear direction.

Spiritual or faith-based values emerge from the Wisdom of God. Gleaned from the pages of scripture and nurtured within the context of Christian community, spiritual values provide a type of connecting tissue between people of faith. Core Christian values are the ones that appear—or should appear—in the personal value systems of those who follow Christ.

Compassion is one such value. It grows out of God's *hesed* (remember that God-word from earlier in this chapter?). Psalm 145:8-10 puts it well: "The LORD is gracious and merciful, slow to anger and abounding in steadfast love. The LORD is good to all, and his compassion is over all that he has made. All your works shall give thanks to you, O LORD, and all your faithful shall bless you."

God has compassion on us. Despite our imperfect tendencies to stray, misbehave, become distracted, and focus inward, God's heart goes out to us. Compassion means, literally, "with passion or love." God's love holds us in orbit and refuses to let us go. Divine compassion fuels God's acts of forgiveness, healing, redemption, and restoration. Jesus's ministry demonstrated as much. More than once, scripture tells us that Jesus had compassion for the hungry, broken-hearted, and suffering people (see Matt. 9:36;14:14; 15:32;20:34; Mk 6:34; 8:2; Lk 7:13; 15:20.) What is more, Jesus's compassion drives his response. He reaches out, acknowledges, cares for, and heals us.

If compassion lies at the heart of God's dealing with us, then it is a value of great worth and something for us to not only treasure but also to emulate. When we put compassion in a central place in our value system, we are taking steps to walk in the wisdom of God.

In a harsh and cold world, where things burst apart without much care, compassion is sorely needed. Compassion opens the heart to the breaks and fissures of those around us that we might too readily pass over in our daily scurry. We see with subversive eyes that dare to view life as it is, beyond the illusions, deceptions, and sugar coating of a culture that lusts after perfection.

It needs mentioning that this isn't easy, and can even be dangerous. Courage is required because when we open our hearts, we become vulnerable to the pain and suffering of others. To do this, we have to cast off the protective coating of our hearts, which leaves them susceptible to being broken and made heavy by the burdens of a hurting world. Once we see, we can't avoid responding. Compassion may start in our heart, but soon it is directing our hands and feet to action. We become a part of God's work of restoration and healing.

Claiming compassion as a core value during a time of transition can have an added benefit: it can be a source of new purpose and direction. Seeing the needs of others with our heart and then reaching out to them with acts of kindness can open new possibilities. Instead of being alone, we will find ourselves in community with others in a way that we've never been before.

A NOTE TO MY SON:

Dear Noah,

Let compassion be a guiding value in your day. Have the courage to see with your heart. For a moment, suspend your scientific mind. Although there is no optic nerve connected to your heart, it has the ability—if you use it—to see in a way that is deeper than our eyes will allow. When you look at another person with your heart, you gaze into their struggles, hurts, and dreams. Heart vision provides more than information; it will move you toward doing something about it. Now, you can't fix or heal most things. You can, however, be present and walk with the other person. In short, you can be a friend.

I know you know this. I've seen you demonstrate compassion. It is a value you lived in the past and which has made you into the caring person that you are today. Please don't forget it. Your heart and the hearts of others will be glad that you remembered.

Love you always,
Dad

A PRAYER FOR YOU:

Gracious God, the source of all compassion, your love is steadfast and endless. You reach out to a hurting world with healing that passes all understanding. Be present in my heart this day so that I might see through the lens of love. Strengthen my failing courage so that I might be humble and vulnerable enough to connect with those who are struggling and in need. Allow your compassion to embolden my response. Through Jesus Christ, amen.

Worship with Everything Ya Got!

Hiking out of a canyon can be exhausting. At the start of the journey, when you have your most energy and enthusiasm, you go down the trail. Gravity helps. Though the descent can be tough on your knees and calves, the rest of your body willingly participates in going deeper. But you must exercise caution and restraint. There is a truism that canyon hikers extol: what goes down must come up!

On your way out of the natural ditch, the task is exponentially harder. Now tired, you need to reach deep within yourself. On the hike back up, when gravity is not your friend, you have to summon strength and focus with your whole body, mind, and spirit—all ya got!

There is a similar experience at the end of a long-distance race. You get tired after running for a couple of miles. Your strength wanes. For that final push to the finish line, you need to concentrate and find the courage to keep going.

When life changes on us, the journey metaphors of canyon hiking and distance running are highly applicable. Grief, which always comes when we lose the people and patterns of life that are familiar to us, makes a body weary. We are en route to a new place, but the canyon rim or finish line is still far off. The struggle tempts us to stop and not go any further. But we can't quit. So we press on through the general confusion and uncertainty of being in a place where things are different. Amidst it all, making decisions can be a particular challenge.

My experiences with distance running and canyon hiking have taught me that when a trail requires me to make difficult decisions at a moment's notice, I need to rely on my inner sense of right and wrong. I need to make a quick withdrawal from my ethics bank.

Shared social values, natural law, experience, and generally accepted moral principles all come together to form our ethics. As Christians, our faith also plays a critical role. Although a constant work in progress, ethics are more fixed than not. We may apply a particular ethic in different ways, depending on a situation. Still, ethics are not easily changed based on a whim or even a feeling. Ethics guide us; they are among the few constants in our life.

In each chapter of this book, I will hold up a different ethical principle that can not only help drive our decisions but also inform our sense of right and wrong. Since we are focusing in this chapter on God, it is fitting that our first driving ethic centers on the foundational relationship that we have with God.

God created us and gave us life. Scripture invites our proper response to be "all in." As the created, we are expected to worship the Creator with all that we have. It lies at the heart of all the commandments: Love the

LORD your God with all your heart, mind, and soul. In short, let all your being give praise and acknowledge God as God.

When we do this, we recognize our place in the big picture. We are not God, nor are we at the center of the universe. This understanding drives an ethic that refuses to elevate our needs and concern above all others. We are part of a more massive creation. Our wants are not placed above all other desires (or needs) because we think that would be a good idea. We are not the end of every means, nor are we the means of every end.

When we put God at the center, our ethics and decision making are no longer stuck on what is best for us. With humility, we seek to honor God. With thanksgiving, we acknowledge that life is full of blessings that we can only correctly understand as gifts. With acts of worship, we orient ourselves in a right relationship with our Creator.

At the moment we find ourselves in the heat of a day, or at the breaking point of a journey, our pretensions of being at the center of the universe fade away. Through frailty, imperfections, exhaustion, and vulnerability we claim our place as creatures of a loving God. We seek entrance into a right relationship with God and discover that not only does that relationship already exist, but God has already been carrying us along.

A NOTE TO MY SON:

Dear Noah,

What I'm about to say is said with the greatest love: You are not at the center of the universe. Neither am I. The center belongs to God. When you accept this truth, things change. You become more humble and more grateful. You will see life a little more like a gift. You will be less likely to demand that everything, every day, needs to go according to your wishes and desires.

When you find yourself tired and weary, when the day is getting to be a little too much to bear, remember to continue your praise and worship of the God at the center of all life. Hard as it might be, recall that God formed your very being, loves you, and wants you to live in a right relationship with others. As you make decisions, consider not only yourself; wonder what others might need and be as generous as you can.

Love you always,
Dad

A PRAYER FOR YOU:

Gracious God, give me the wisdom to worship you above all things. Guide my actions so that I might give all I have in praise of you. Help me when I struggle to make a decision. Let me consider others before myself. Empower my response, generosity, compassion, and kindness. Through Jesus Christ, amen.

A Prayer for Busy Feet

It was a problem. The pastor was too busy to pray. On most days, he scurried from task to task, ministry to ministry, person to person without taking much time to breathe, not to mention pray. Sure, the hurried cleric would pray a bit along the way, but it was always on behalf of others. In a typical day, there might be a dozen prayers that he'd craft on the spot as he cycled through a packed schedule. Prayer was one of the tools he used in the spiritual care of those he was called to serve. It wasn't that the prayers lacked sincerity; they were down to earth and came from a place of conviction and faith. Ironically, though, the one who found the time to pray with everyone else at a moment's notice couldn't find a moment to pray for himself.

More than once, the pastor tried to adopt a morning prayer regimen. But the pressing matters of each day soon exerted a gravitational pull thwarting all intentions of starting the day in prayer. Determined to pray, he tried to pray at bedtime instead. Unfortunately, within moments of shutting the lights off and closing his eyes, sleep caused the frustrated pastor's prayers to go uncompleted.

Despite numerous attempts at trying to make time for personal prayer, the pastor's inability caused guilt to linger and fester. There were even times when this professional provider of prayer felt like a fraud. There was a spiritual void in his personal prayer life.

I know this story all too well. I'm embarrassed to say that I was that pastor who prayed with everyone else but could never seem to make the time to pray myself. I was too busy. At times, I was overwhelmed with the multiple demands and burdens of ministry. I was too tired, and my heart was running too many races that were heading in opposite directions.

At other times, the fast pace of my multi-tasking life was a form of intoxication. I delighted in getting so much accomplished. It was back in the day that I wore my "super-pastor" cape with a sense of misplaced pride. Look at all I was getting done. God must be so proud of me! Time to shift gears again; what's next?

How about you? What place does prayer occupy in your life? Do you have a routine? Do you pray regularly? Or do you only pray in times of crisis? Does the pace of life dictate how and when you pray or don't pray? Do you feel guilt or embarrassment for not living up to personal expectations? Maybe you don't feel much at all when it comes to praying. Is it awkward?

Over the years, I have developed a variety of prayer practices that have helped me to move from where I was in my praying to a healthier place. In the coming chapters, I'll share a few of these unique ways of praying in the hope that they might be a resource for you. These practices come from my desire to be more active in prayer as a child of God.

Prayer is about connection. When we pray, we recognize that God is a part of our lives and that we are in a relationship with our Creator. We acknowledge, through prayer, that God is active in our lives even when we can't fully understand that connection.

Prayer is also an intentional turning toward God. As such, it is an act of repentance. Busy lives distract us from paying attention to God. Our ability to multi-task deludes us into thinking that we can do all that we need to do, at all times. Prayer seeks an honesty and vulnerability within ourselves. It acknowledges a deep need for God's help, guidance, and strength.

Because life is complicated, fast-paced, and uneven, I have found that no one particular way of praying works for me all the time. On some days, and under certain circumstances, I pray in certain ways. On other days, I pray differently. Sometimes I feel like my prayers are working to connect me with the presence of God in my life. Sometimes they don't. When that happens, I shift practices. When I sense that my prayer is not turning my focus on God but rather swirling all about me, I'll try a new style. Although I have my favorite go-to methods of prayer, I'm open to innovation.

A few years back, I stumbled upon a practice involving shoes. It was right in the midst of the flurry that I described above. It was early in the morning and I needed to leave the house while it was still dark outside, though I can't recall exactly why I was up so early. Dressed for action, I had located my shoes after my usual hunt.

Sitting on the bottom step of the stairs that led up to the bedrooms of my two-story house, I was feeling a little frazzled. I held a shoe in my hands and for some reason stopped. Taking a deep breath, I looked at the sole. I then proceeded to pray. I asked God for the strength to guide my feet so that I might walk in love and grace. With that, my shoe-prayer practice began.

Try it out. When you put your shoes on tomorrow morning, pause for a moment. Hold your shoe, sneaker, boot, or sandal in your hand. Take a deep breath. Think ahead to your day and where you are likely to walk. Think about the people and situations you are likely to encounter. Ask God for guidance and to direct your steps. Seek God's blessing upon your footwear. Be intentional about taking God with you into your day.

God is going to be there anyway, but it makes a world of difference if we open ourselves to God's presence.

A NOTE TO MY SON:

Dear Noah,

Between walking to classes and marching in the band, I'm sure your feet are getting quite the workout these days. I hope your sneakers are holding up. No doubt you are busy. It may not seem like there are enough hours to get it all done. Years ago, I thought that it would be great if someone could add a few more hours to the day. Wouldn't that be cool? It wouldn't work, though. I would use up any additional hours and be no further ahead. We don't need more time. We need to make better use of the time we have.

That brings me to mention the need to take some time to pray. It doesn't have to be long or wordy. A deep breath and a pause will do. When you put your well-worn sneakers on today, stop and take a brief moment with God.

Walk well wherever your travels might take you.

Love you always,
Dad

A PRAYER FOR YOU:

As you put on your footwear today, stop and hold it in your hands. You are free to use these words or others like them.

Dear God, bless these shoes. Be with me along the path of this day. Guide my steps according to your love and grace. Let me feel the strength of your presence as I interact with others and encounter both challenges and opportunities. Through Jesus Christ, amen.

CHAPTER THREE

CREATION

Our first family camping trip out West was to the Badlands in South Dakota. Katie and I were still living in New Jersey at the time, so it took us three full days to drive to this natural wonderland. I wanted my boys to see the mighty buffalo and the beauty of Western spaces. My parents did this for me, and I felt it essential to continue the tradition.

Not only did we watch a herd of buffalo, which was bigger than the boys could count, but we had a fantastic time among the buttes, pinnacles, and spires of Badlands National Park. Erosion plays such a role in the constant shaping of that landscape. It is a truly fascinating place that always seems to capture my imagination anew. I believe that it also helped to foster in my kids an appreciation of nature and the great outdoors.

Nature is the quintessential teacher. As spectacular as the photographs might be, they are no substitute for being there in person. To look with your eyes, to breathe in the air, and to walk down paths leading to wild places is an experience unlike any digital representation. Human creatures were designed to interact with the broader creation using all our available senses.

In our techno-centric culture, there is a danger of losing connection with the rest of God's handiwork. Virtual reality, with its increasing refinement, has assumed a more significant place in our lives than was previously imagined by even the most outrageous of science fictions. Young and old spend more hours watching pixilated images than they do engaging the real world.

Although technology offers benefits for connecting friends and family who are separated by distance, it has also caused families to place their focus elsewhere. How many times have you been to a restaurant and seen families eating in silence, each on their electronic device? Sadly, technology has played a negative role in distorting and dividing creation into unnatural segments.

All of this has implications for our spiritual lives. In this chapter, we will be focusing on creation. As we seek wisdom to face changes and transitions in life, we must look to the larger world that God made, which is in a continual state of change and evolution. We will look at developing a theology of creation that can equip us to interact with the beauty, fragility, and harshness of the natural world.

Our Jesus story will invite us to ponder what it means to have Christ as co-Creator. Using a tiny seed and a massive ocean, we will stretch our spiritual imagination. When we turn to values and ethics, we'll move in the direction of stewardship and care of creation. Finally, our prayer practice will involve a walk in the woods.

When we interact with the world beyond our screens and devices, we are taking a step toward understanding that we are but a part of a greater whole. God created all of life to be in right relationships and *shalom*. Although a pervasive brokenness clouds this vision, the restoration and redemption of the entire creation remains God's dream. Seeking communion with life beyond ourselves, we can tap into God's hope for life. As we participate in God's hopes and dreams through our choices and actions, we will find new purpose and meaning for the future.

A NOTE TO MY SON:

Dear Noah,

Remember when we went to the Badlands? Your brother and you climbed all over! It was a fun place filled with many wonders and beauty. Recall the buffalo that surrounded our car and walked right past us to graze on the prairie grass? We hung out the windows of the old truck to get a better look at them.

Whether we travel far or near, we can see evidence of the beautiful world that God created. Be sure to notice the nature on your campus. Look at it with scientific curiosity and spiritual reverence. Think about how you can help out the creation through your choices and actions.

Love you always,
Dad

A PRAYER FOR YOU:

Creator God, there is a beauty and wonder that we can find in your creation. Give us the wisdom to look, the ability to perceive, and the strength to join in your work of caretaking and restoration. Through Jesus Christ, amen.

Bara and Ktizo

One of my perpetual hobbies involves working with wood. More than once, I have professed my affinity for the making of sawdust. There are piles of wood chips and dust in my garage that bear witness to my proficiency at cutting and grinding wood into bits.

From as early as I can remember, I have enjoyed making things with my hands. I gain great satisfaction from looking at something that I've put together. Before my efforts, it was a stack of wood. Now it has shape, form, and function.

Part of what makes us human beings is our ability to dream, design, solve problems, and build stuff. Whether the goal of our work is an artistic expression or to satisfy a human need such as housing or transportation, human creatures are makers and producers. We have agency and ability to transform our environment, ease our struggles, or lift our spirits. Moreover, we use and develop tools to accomplish a great many tasks.

Over millennia, human creatures and societies have progressed from bands of nomadic hunter/gatherers to complex and interconnected civilizations that span the globe. Through ingenuity and invention, we have explored and forever changed the land, sea, air, and space. Is there no end to our progress? No limit to what we can do?

It would be good to stop right about now, before this becomes propaganda for a new ride at Disney's Epcot Center celebrating human progress. Lest we get caught up in the pep rally, there is also a broken side to human creation that, if taken into account , at least questions the narrative of steady human progress.

We humans haven't always used our minds, skills, and efforts for good. If the twentieth century teaches us anything, it is that the works of our hands can be evil and lead to unimaginable destruction. Nations hold the ability to annihilate each other and forever destroy the planet. Greed drives consumption and pollution that benefits the few at the expense of the many. Although we have the ability to provide enough food to feed the hungry across the globe, we lack the will to do so, and children starve to death.

Closer to home, we don't always use our hands to help others because they are often too busy taking care of ourselves, acquiring things for our own benefit instead of working for the good of those around us. Or worse yet, we are too busy in little virtual ghettos of our construction that we don't even notice those around us in the first place. Our materialistic culture—also a byproduct of our own actions—has drained us spiritually and deluded us into thinking that we are the creators. We have made ourselves into an image of God.

Scripture makes a distinction when it talks about creation. *Bara* (in the Old Testament) and *Ktizo* (in the New Testament) are Hebrew and Greek words, respectively, used exclusively to describe God's activity. Put plainly, only God "creates." In contrast, humans "make" or "fashion" things. We are not the only creatures who do this. Animals and plants produce milk or grain. But creatures don't create life from nothingness. Only the Creator has that power.

Why is this distinction important? It helps to bring some order into the chaos of our culture's blasphemous deification of the self. Claiming power that is God's alone is at the root of our brokenness, violence, pollution, and desecration of creation. Identifying God as Creator and us as creatures leans in the direction of right relationships. God gives us life. All that we have comes as a blessing to which we can only say "thank you." Awe and respect are the proper response for us to offer God.

Following the life of Jesus, we share gratitude through sharing love and kindness with others. We can use our creativity and the working of our hands to do this in all sorts of ways. Each of us brings unique gifts to bear. In the process, we turn from usurpers to participants in what God is doing to bring about the restoration and renewal of creation.

When this happens, something inside us shifts. Instead of seeking power that is not ours, we direct our efforts to embrace our created selves. Gone is the fabricated need to be a god or in control; these are illusions that can only frustrate us. In its place is a sense of peace that comes from accepting and acknowledging our "creature-ness." Though we are fragile and vulnerable creatures, we belong to our Creator, who continues to love us and delight in our lives. We are the work of God's hands, which create us anew. It is out of this relationship that we are invited to build our lives.

A NOTE TO MY SON:
Dear Noah,

I know that you brought a toolbox with you to your dorm room. No doubt you have already used it to fix something, tighten some screw, or work on your bike. You are good with your hands and at solving problems. Engineering seems like a good fit for you.

Even if you didn't have a knack for such things, it would still be good for you to put your hands, head, and heart to work. Everyone needs to engage all three areas, for we are living in critical times. From the ecological destruction of the planet to an unkind word whispered behind someone's back, there are a lot of things that are threatening life in big and small ways. All hands, heads, and hearts are needed to work toward good.

It may seem overwhelming. Remember: the journey of a thousand miles begins with a single step. Today, you can take a step in God's direction of love. In the short run, it may not seem like much. In the long term, it will make all the difference in your life.

Love you always,
Dad

A PRAYER FOR YOU:

Creator God, you alone can create life. You formed me inside and out. Your breath fills my lungs and animates my being. Help me to focus on you and give thanks to you for your abundant blessings. Let me be generous so that I might put to good use the gifts, talents, and time that come from you. Empower me to participate in your ongoing work of restoration and renewal. Through Jesus Christ, amen.

Co-Creating Christ

"In the beginning was the Word, and the Word was with God, and the Word was God. He was in the beginning with God. All things came into being through him, and without him not one thing came into being. What has come into being in him was life, and the life was the light of all people. The light shines in the darkness, and the darkness did not overcome it."

— John 1:1-5

It has been many years since I've needed to put a chair next to the drill press in my garage workshop. This piece of furniture, which came from my grandfather's apartment, provided a platform on which my preschooler would stand. Noah, decked out in tot-sized overalls and wearing his safety goggles, learned how to use a drill press around the time he was learning his alphabet. Together we'd build stuff with our hands. We continue to share this passion.

Recently, I've taken up a new pastime with my other son, Mark, who is a gifted artist. With sketchbooks in hand, we head off to the Minnesota Zoo, where we have a membership. We wander through the zoological park until some creature sparks our interest. Carefully, we observe the animal's form. We then sketch it. It is a bunch of fun. Already our sketchbooks contain numerous pages documenting our zoo adventures.

Creating art and other projects with both my boys brings me great pleasure. I get to see both their perspectives come out in the works of their hands. Although we are working together to accomplish a similar task, I am amazed at how differently we approach or view things. I learn a lot from them and am grateful for their willingness to create with me.

The Gospel writer, John, begins his narrative of Jesus's life in a bold place. John asserts that Jesus was present at the very start of creation. Not only present, but also participating in the act of creation itself. It is a scandalous concept! Recall, in the mind of the ancient authors of scripture, the act of creation was reserved for God alone. Establishing Jesus as a co-Creator, John points to the eternal aspect of Jesus's divine nature.

It is the highest Christology that we encounter in any of the Gospels. Jesus is present alongside the Father, and together they create *all* life. The good, bad, and even the ugly come into being as a result of their combined act of creation. As a result, the relationship that exists between all life (human, animal, and plant) and its Creator includes not only the Father but also the Son.

Wow! It is a mind-blowing thing. When it comes to God, it is easy to get lost in mystery and majesty. Creation is vast. Despite humanity's efforts to explore, chart, and understand life, we have not even scratched the surface. There is so much that lies beyond our comprehension. How can we begin to imagine the Source of all life? It defies our greatest knowledge.

On the other, we know something about Jesus. We have stories of his life. From an early age, we have learned of Jesus's compassion, kindness, inclusiveness, generosity, and hospitality. He healed broken lives and welcomed children as a sign of God's kingdom. Jesus sought out regenerative relationships with those who needed them most. He proclaimed God's forgiveness where there was a separation between folks and God, folks and their neighbor.

By identifying Jesus as a co-Creator of creation, John invites us to consider not only the unknowable, mysterious God but also the revealed Christ. The love and grace of Jesus had a role in the creation of life. The compassion and hospitality of Christ were there and left a mark, as all artisans leave a trademark on the work of their hands. From the furthest unknown star in the sky to the smallest crawling thing on the ground to that grumpy guy who lives down the street, all were formed by the hands of our divine carpenter.

It raises a holy question: How can such things be? If Jesus—who we know is full of grace and mercy—had a role in creating all that lives and has being, then there must be a trace element of Christ in all creation. If that is so, then even the one I have labeled as my enemy or "unlovable" is connected to Christ. I am forced to rethink a few of my biases and prejudices. No longer can I claim special favored status as a child of God, for *all* people, by the very nature of their existence, are also children of God. The love that I experience as a child of God is available to all others.

This understanding begins to change the way I relate to those outside my experience and religious tradition. Instead of forcing my faith on others, so that they might know God in the same way that I've come to know God, I need to take a step back. What might I learn about God/Christ from the non-Christian? What insight might even the atheist provide as I reach out in love to them?

I'm now thinking of the rich experience of working and creating with my boys. I've learned so much from them. They see things differently. Sure, I have skills to share and teach them, but I don't have that market cornered. Through our relationship, they have taught me a great deal about life and love. I'm always looking forward to our next project and the fantastic opportunity for growth that I know it will contain.

A NOTE TO MY SON:
Dear Noah,

I miss building things with you. The other day, Mark and I went to the zoo to draw. He misses you too! We spent some time at the monkey enclosure sketching those rascals. They were bouncing off the proverbial walls, and all the literal ones as well. Boy, are they tough to draw. Always in motion. Mark did a better job of capturing them in his sketchbook. Give me a sloth any day, I say.

Back to the workshop. I was puttering around there making a few things. They came out better than my monkey drawings. Still, it would have been great to have you there. I appreciate your skill, insight, and extra hands. I'm already lining up a few projects for when you come home at the next break.

In the meantime, I hope you find a creative outlet for your hands. What is more, I hope you take advantage of an opportunity to create something with someone else. Working together with others can be frustrating; there are always compromises to work out and quirks to figure out. It can also be a rewarding experience as you navigate differences and encounter different perspectives. You might even learn something about yourself or God that you never knew before! Imagine that.

Love you always,
Dad

A PRAYER FOR YOU:

Creator, through the love of Christ, you brought my life into being—not only my life, but all life. Give me the wisdom to seek your presence in all that I might encounter today. Let me learn about your love and grace from the numerous encounters of this day. Guide me to share your love actively in all I do. Through Jesus Christ, amen.

Beautiful, Brittle, and Brutal

About forty or so of us were squeezed into the bathroom. Men, women, and even a few dogs. The concrete bathhouse was the designated storm shelter, and according to the weather warning that popped up on everybody's phones, it was the place to go. Our motorhomes, trailers, tents, and vehicles would offer little safety should the hurricane winds come off the Gulf and make landfall along the Florida coast. For well over an hour, we sat on the floor and benches to wait out the storm.

Earlier in the day, my family had toured the Sarasota area. It was beautiful. The beaches, palm trees, and blue water were instantly relaxing. What an incredible place for a vacation! At a seafood restaurant, nestled in a small fishing harbor, local pelicans greeted us with noble gazes while the seagulls attempted to steal our lunch. There was nothing at the time to indicate that we would be spending a portion of the night crowded with our new best friends into a campground bathroom.

From my travels and experiences, I've encountered three contradictory aspects of creation. Creation is certainly beautiful. I could go on and on attempting extolling creation's beauty. From lofty mountain summits to rolling waves crashing along a tropical beach; from the solid biomass of rainforests to saguaro cacti standing tall in the desert heat; from frozen lakes to underground caverns, there are so many wonders to experience in the natural world that will take your breath away. The hymnist Carl Boberg got it right: "How Great Thou Art!" If my failing language could accurately describe the beauty of creation (which it can't), I'd only be conveying a portion of the story.

Creation is also brittle. Throughout the natural world, you encounter a delicate balance. Sometimes just a few degrees of temperature change can have devastating consequences on entire ecosystems. From fauna to flora, life often struggles for survival. Whether we're huddling for protection in a storm shelter or visiting a loved one in intensive care, we know all too well that life is fragile and needs protection, healing, and restoration. The brokenness that pervades creation brings me to the third descriptor: brutal.

Yes, creation is also brutal. Consider the natural disasters and storms that threaten everything in their path. In the animal world, survival of the fittest is the law of the jungle. In the human world, many subscribe to the same philosophy; consider the injustice, violence, and hard side of life. And then there are the illnesses that claim the lives of so many people, good people whom we love. Although we may not want to admit it, when it comes to the natural world, the thorns can be as large as the flower.

Where is God in all three of these areas? We probably have no problem identifying the fingerprints of God in a golden sunset over the ocean or on a crisp autumn day. Who doesn't feel sacred wonder when they stand at the rim of a canyon or atop a mountain summit? It is harder to recognize God's presence in the brittle and brutal.

Here lies a dilemma. If God creates everything in creation, then why is so much broken? Is God careless or reckless in making things that break and fall apart before the warranty period runs out? Or worse, is there a lack of compassion at the heart of the hidden Creator of the universe? Maybe even a harshness or brutality? Is God inherently good, or is that just the side we see when we look at Jesus? Could there be a dark side to God?

Christian theologians over the centuries have pointed to human sin as the cause of all turmoil and tribulation. The Creator is not to blame for the brittle and brutal—it is the fault of a wayward creation. Our disregard for life and misuse of the natural world has resulted in death and destruction. We, not God, are responsible for the downside and dark turns that we experience in life.

This much is true—our pollution of waterways and excessive deforestation have had a negative impact on the planet. But what about natural disasters? Even if human consumption didn't escalate the magnitude of these events, they would still occur. Storms are brutal regardless of mortal sin.

What about the extinction of species? Again, humans have had an amplifying effect on the disappearance of life forms such as has not been experienced prior. That said, processes of natural selection function based on creatures not being able to survive in a harsh or changing environment. Sin fails as a catch-all explanation for the fragility of life found in each eon. But if sin is only a partial answer, how do we wrap our heads around the brittle and brutal nature of creation?

I must be honest. As often as I've tried to make sense of it, I've come up empty. Though I never expected easy answers, even the complicated answers elude me. I know why some give up the God-search when faced with brittle and brutal reality. It is hard not to fall into the pit of despair and become jaded when talking about the difficult aspects of spirituality and faith. What good is a belief system if it cannot stop bad things from happening?

When faced with such thoughts, I find myself drawn to the wisdom of the cross. I may not be able to scratch the surface on the hidden nature of God, but I have this story about Jesus's willingness to enter the brittle and brutal side of life. On the cross, Jesus experiences the very worst that life has to offer. If you want to know where God is during the brittle and brutal moments, the cross says to look into the brokenness and tension. Look for God in the places where life breaks down and things don't add up. Seek divine presence in the hurt, despair, and jaded moments.

Granted, this doesn't answer why creation is so brittle and brutal. Nevertheless, knowing that God remains with us when tragedy hits can be a tremendous comfort. It gives us the strength to carry on. What is more, there is hope. If the Creator, who brought the first light into the darkness of primordial chaos, is with us in our shadowed moments, then there is the possibility that light will shine anew. Faith alone can navigate these choppy spiritual waters.

It is a bumpy boat ride that we all take. Sometimes the waves are more significant than at other times. When that happens, we need to hold on for dear life. And then there are times when we just need to wait in the storm shelter until the skies are once again clear.

A NOTE TO MY SON:

Dear Noah,

Already you know that life isn't always joyful. There are moments (sometimes even weeks) when things don't go your way. You will see that life can be fragile and unfair. At these times, you might be angry at God. How could God let !$%@!#$ happen?

God wants you to be honest. If you are angry and disappointed, then be sure to include those emotions in your prayer. Don't avoid your negative thoughts. Rest assured, if God put up with Moses, God will tolerate your tantrums.

Be sure, too, to look for God in the midst of your storm, mess, and nightmare. Seek glimpses of God's grace and love. Search for the peace that passes your understanding. The promise that the cross makes is that God is not going anywhere when things get tough. Instead, God will be in a spot where the fire is hottest and the manure is thickest. Trust me, I've been there and got the T-shirt!

Love you always,
Dad

A PRAYER FOR YOU:

Gracious God, you are always present in life. Give me the vision to recognize your life-giving presence in not only the beauty of creation but also in the brittle and brutal places. Allow the cross of Jesus to remind me that your love remains in the midst of struggle and death. Through Jesus Christ, amen.

Walking with Humility

After hours of travel, we finally pulled into the parking lot of the Giant Forest in Sequoia National Park. Already, our eyes had feasted upon the sight of some of the most massive living things on the planet: the giant sequoia trees.

These ancient creatures defy measurement by the eyes. Located in the grove of the Giant Forest is the granddaddy of them all: the General Sherman tree. At 275 feet tall and 25 feet in diameter, this 2,300- to 2,700-year-old tree is referred to by some as the biggest living thing on the planet.

Walking through the Giant Forest, which houses dozens of other giant sequoias, was a humbling experience. Some of these trees had been alive since before the time

Jesus walked on the earth. Imagine that! They were thousands of years old. Not only that, but you couldn't even see the top (or crown, if you are a botanist.) With neck strained backward, you had to be careful you didn't walk into something.

Wow. Look at that one! And that one! That is how we went along. With each step, anticipation built. It didn't seem like anything was going to be bigger than what we had already seen.

Finally, we made it to the base of the tree named after the American Civil War general. At the bottom of this giant, an overwhelming sense of awe washed over me. I was staring at something that I couldn't wrap my imagination around, never mind my arms.

I resisted the urge to kneel, which is what I would have done if I were by myself. I didn't want to embarrass the rest of my family, who had tolerated the long car trip to see a tree. But what is one to do when in the presence of something *spectacular?* Like an audience with the monarchs of old, the experience demanded respect and a show of humility.

It wasn't the first time I'd felt like that in my journeys to visit natural wonders. Time and again, creation has a humbling effect on my spirit. In silent adoration, I look with eyes linked to the innermost part of my heart. It doesn't take long before I begin to offer praise to the Creator who formed such magnificence.

Humility is a critical value to glean and claim from our interaction with creation. Not that it is all that popular or prized within our culture. The pundits of "make it your best day" have so directed our attention inward that we are not likely to give up our false place at the center of the universe. According to today's dominant consumer-based value system, life is all about what you want and desire. Of course, everybody can't get all they want, so there is incessant competition: I have to fight to get what I deserve or to keep what I have acquired.

It was this struggle, combined with the lust and greed of an industrializing nation, that caused saws to destroy what centuries of fires, drought, and adverse conditions couldn't topple, felling the grand redwoods. Sadly, a cultivated humility is absent at the heart of the history of human disregard for the natural order.

Claiming a humble approach to living is essential. It is a necessary corrective if we want to depart from the path of assured destruction. Our culture can't continue indefinitely down the road of consumption. Eventually, there will be no more trees left in the forest if we don't cease unrestrained lumbering; the same goes for all the other resources with which we are blessed.

Alone, I may not be able to stem the tide of cultural pride and arrogance. I can, however, choose to be humble myself. Through my decisions and actions, I can show honor and respect for all the life that surrounds me. An excellent place to start is to recognize that all of life—from the tiniest gnat to the mighty sequoia—is created by God. What is more, God remains connected to us through a delicate and not-fully-understood relationship with all life. There is a sacredness to it all that we ought not to miss.

It would do our spirits well to enter each day with a sense of reverence. Perhaps kneeling at the base of a giant tree isn't such a crazy idea after all. Maybe we pause with morning coffee in hand and look out the window at a bird on a branch. Or we rise a little earlier to see the sunrise.

Through recognition and appreciation of the world beyond ourselves, we will nurture within us the value of humility. We claim the truth that we are part of something much bigger than our needs and wants. We are not the most important part, either.

When we are humble, we actively live into our created selves—we head in the direction of becoming the person God created. Here we find a sense of peace that passes our understanding and defies our manipulation. We can rest in being God's children and stop running on the treadmill of trying to be something we are not.

A NOTE TO MY SON:
Dear Noah,

Remember General Sherman? Not the historic general with the tousled hair and shifty eye, but the tree? Remember the day that we hiked to the base of that ancient giant and saw the biggest thing (that we know) on the planet? I will let you in on a little, embarrassing secret; if there wasn't a fence around it, I might have hugged it. I know, my arms wouldn't have fit, but it would have been worth trying anyway. I was just so happy to be there and to be there with you, your mother, and your brother.

I was also experiencing a sense of being in the presence of something greater than my life. That feeling is called "humility," and it is a good one to feel. When we are humble, we accept that we are not the center of the universe. God alone should be in that privileged location. Why is this important?

When we think too highly of ourselves, we are apt to do stupid things like cut down ancient trees to make toothpicks, or treat others poorly. It messes up our lives and the life of the whole planet.

Continue to walk in the way of humility, knowing that God loves you (as do your parents and your whole family) even if you aren't the most important thing out there.

Love you always,
Dad

A PRAYER FOR YOU:

Gracious God, you alone are at the center of life. Let me walk a humble path today. Fill me with reverence, respect, and gratitude so that I might recognize and honor the created work of your hands. Through Jesus Christ, amen.

To Till and Keep the Garden

Although we always lived in and near densely populated urban areas, my dad had a backyard garden. There, he would grow tomatoes, peppers, snap peas, rhubarb, cucumbers, zucchini, and eggplant, among other things. Each night of the summer, still in his work clothes, Dad would go putter in the garden. Sometimes I would help; other times he was by himself. The fresh produce was a real treat. I'm convinced that there is nothing quite like a homegrown tomato.

On the counter in my kitchen is a bowl full of tomatoes and cucumbers that my wife, Katie, picked from our garden. It is that time of the year: the vegetables are in, and in abundance. Having a backyard garden plot, even a small one like we do, is a blessing. Not only does it produce wonders for the table, but tending and tilling does fantastic things for the soul. I think I finally understand now why Dad gardened. It wasn't just for the vegetables—though they helped out a hungry family's grocery bill. It was about an inner need to till and keep a garden. It satisfied a desire to plant and watch something as it grows. It allowed him to be a caretaker.

This role has biblical roots. In the second story of creation, found in Genesis, Chapter 2, God creates humanity to be gardeners. Right at the start, we learn that there was a problem. There was soil, but no one to "till the ground (Genesis 2:5)." The seeds of plants and herbs were in the field waiting for the rain to fall. God had planted the garden, but someone needed to take care of it. So God created the human creature to be a gardener, to till and keep the tomatoes and cucumbers, to make sure the zucchini didn't get out of hand. "The LORD God took the man and put him in the garden of Eden to till it and keep it (Genesis 2:15)."

Of course, what happens next is that the human creature messes it all up. Instead of living out his calling to be a good steward and tend to the garden, Adam seeks to manipulate and dominate. He, along with his partner Eve, try to usurp God's power and eat from the restricted tree of the knowledge of good and evil. This was a subversive and sinful act that led to their expulsion from the garden paradise.

We can tell the story of Adam and Eve to describe how brokenness and suffering have entered the human experience. Through its simple plot of disobedience, we lament paradise lost. Here is why we struggle in life: we had it made but didn't follow the rules. See where that gets you? One moral lapse of judgment forever marks humanity.

Of course, humanity continues to excel at disregarding God's ways. Sin is a plentiful harvest that we continue to bring in from the field. Brokenness permeates our relationships with God, each other, and the earth. It doesn't take an environmentalist to know that we have done a great deal of damage to this garden planet. Ironically, misinterpretation of the "dominate and subdue" directive of the first creation story (Genesis, Chapter 1) fueled our consumptive and destructive behavior. We have gone beyond taming the wilderness to pursue strip mining, deforestation, and pollution. If we don't stop the madness, the harm might be irreversible.

How far we have come from God's original intent! Let's go back to that beautiful second story of creation involving the garden. Before sin enters and dominates the narrative, there is simply the garden. God had a garden that needs someone to care for it, so God created us. It is in our nature to be caretakers of creation. From this understanding grows an ethic of stewardship.

Stewardship begins with the recognition that the garden (a metaphor for all life) belongs to God. From the things we can hold in our hands to the next breath that we take into our lungs, everything is a gift that we have for but a time. When you count up the years of life, they are short. We live for a season, perhaps two, and then we return to the earth.

What we do with the gift of life is our choice. We can try to dominate, control, and alter the flow to favor self-interests. Along the way, we might even accumulate power, prestige, and a little privilege. We can choose to consider the effects our actions have on others and the planet, or we can disregard them. But even if we attempt to ignore these effects, how we live has consequences. Walking in the path of destruction is never good and will ultimately extract a dear price.

Throughout scripture, the Bible encourages us to walk in the direction of God. Recognizing that our life belongs to God, we move with thanksgiving into the role of caretaker. Living God's way, we work the soil of relationships. Respect. Honor. Kindness. Mutual love.

These are the tools that our hands need. Beyond the garden metaphor, stewardship involves the actual caretaking of the soil. There is a need for us to get our hands dirty physically. We must move from the abstraction of caring for the planet to actual, hands-on engagement.

Growing vegetables in our backyard, composting table scraps, lessening our carbon imprint, recycling, using fewer plastics, shopping at farmers markets, etc.—all these things are holy endeavors. Each is an ethical application of being a steward of creation. Each moves in the direction of tilling and keeping the earth. Each allows us to claim the role of being a caretaker in God's garden.

A NOTE TO MY SON:

Dear Noah,

Have you seen any of the fresh vegetables that the university grows in the cafeteria line? They are supposed to be there. I was happy to see the effort throughout the campus to recycle, reuse, and compost.

Whenever I see or use a plastic water bottle, I think of you. Throughout high school, you championed the use of reusable water bottles. You gave witness to using fewer plastics, which eventually wind up in landfills or the ocean. As a result of your efforts, we used less plastic as a family.

Did you know that what you were doing was the holy work of tilling and keeping God's garden? Did you know that you were practicing the ethic of stewardship?

I know that you continue to fill your water bottle as you keep hydrated. May you find the strength to stay at your holy gardening. Lord knows that we need your entire generation to become experienced gardeners!

Love you always,
Dad

A PRAYER FOR YOU:

Gracious God, you made a garden and created humanity to be gardeners. Empower me this day to get my hands dirty. Let me work with renewed passion in tilling and keeping so that your garden may flourish and produce abundantly. Through Jesus Christ, amen.

A Walk in the Park

The first prayer practices that I learned as a child involved closing my eyes, folding my hands, and sitting quietly. This introspective method of prayer remains a well-used tool in my box. I am grateful for the way it helps focus me, especially when life is going a hundred miles an hour. Stop. Be still. Seek God's renewing presence. It is good to withdraw a little, from time to time, from the chaos that swirls around.

Yet just like eating nothing but cookie dough ice cream, however good it might be, can be damaging, an exclusive diet of *anything* can have unintended consequences. As calming as it might be, and renewing of our spirit, prayer practices that turn exclusively inward move away from the outside world. Please don't misunderstand me. Connecting our inner selves to God is a good thing to do. But if spirituality lives only in that intimate and private space between God and me, then we are missing something. Faith is not just about Jesus and me. Faith also has an outward dimension that moves outward toward the whole creation. Prayer practices that seek to open us to the God "out there" are beneficial.

Try this out. What is the most natural space near where you live? Is there a patch of woods, a pond, or a park close to you? Put on your most comfortable walking shoes/sneakers and head out. Pause at the start of your designated prayer walk. Close your eyes for a moment. Breathe deeply. Ask for God to walk with you and to open your spirit.

Turn off your cell phone (or at least put it on vibrate). This is a time of prayer. You are seeking to communicate with God; let all other conversations wait for a while. If you are concerned about time, use your phone to set a timer for twenty minutes or half an hour. Commit to whatever time you have available; make your time sacred by setting it aside for the sole purpose of your walking prayer.

Walk. Breathe. Allow your senses to connect you to your surroundings. Smile and gaze upon creation. What do you notice? In what can you take delight? What do you see that is in need of care? What thoughts come to mind? Are you thinking about what you need to pick up from the grocery store for dinner? If so, stop. Now is not the time. Let your mind wander in unfamiliar places: meander across the field to the tree line; follow a bird as it performs acrobatic maneuvers in the sky; revel in the colors of a blooming flower or autumn leaves. Be playful and free as your imagination engages creation.

Ask yourself as you wander along: Where is God in all of this? Where are the fingerprints of the divine? Is there an absence—a place where God doesn't seem to be? Perhaps a location that bears witness more to human brokenness than heavenly origin? Reflect on this as well. Why does it seem to be disconnected from God? What would it take for us to change our perspective? What if God was even in the situations that we deem ungodly?

Employ all your senses during your prayer walk. Don't only see but feel, smell, and (if possible) taste. Appreciate the wholeness of the experience. Seek to glean wisdom from it all. Allow God to interact with you in a different way than you would otherwise expect.

You can even do this kind of prayer in an urban landscape. Seek the signs of growth and life as you walk down a concrete sidewalk. Pray with eyes wide open. Clear your mind of all distractions. Seek God's presence in the hustle and bustle of a city street. What opportunities and challenges to being a child of God do you find there? What blessings are present for you to receive with a sense of gratitude? Pray on the go as you engage a creation that remains in the heart of God.

At the end of your walk—whether you complete your designated path or your timer runs out—pause again. Close your eyes. Breathe deeply. Thank God for the time you have spent together. Later on, you might want to follow up by reflecting on the experience in a journal or on a blog. Or you may choose to let the experience simply be a moment in time that you spent walking with God.

You can repeat this prayer practice as many times as you'd like. There are benefits to retracing your steps along the same path; you will see new things each time. Maybe you'll decide to use the practice as part of walking your dog or on a nightly walk. Be flexible and try different things. If it works for you, you will have gained another way of connecting to God in your overall spiritual journey.

A NOTE TO MY SON:
Dear Noah,

Okay, I have something for you to try. An action prayer. Next time you have about a half-hour free, go for a walk around campus. Follow the directions above for a walking prayer. Pray as you go, with eyes and heart open. Look for signs of God's presence as you wander around the beautiful grounds of your school. If something catches your eye, stay with it. Wonder. Delight in the lovely things you see. Ask yourself, what does God want me to see on this walk? You might be surprised at what you discover. Worst case scenario, you got some good exercise and a chance to get outside.

Love you always,
Dad

A PRAYER FOR YOU:

Gracious God, awaken my senses so that I might connect with you during my daily walks. Guide my steps so that I may travel in your ways. Help me to see that which I usually overlook. Empower my actions so that they might reflect your care and compassion. Through Jesus Christ, amen.

CHAPTER FOUR

EVIL

Things do more than go bump in the night. Sometimes bad things happen to good people. Evil intrudes and invades without much warning. "Like a roaring lion your adversary the devil prowls around, looking for someone to devour (1 Peter 5:8)." Every day, innocent people suffer from car accidents, violence, disease, natural disasters, and so on.

I remember the night all too well. I was on my first overnight rotation during my clinical pastoral education at a level-one trauma center in Newark, New Jersey. I happened to be doing my rounds in the emergency room when the ambulance brought in a teenager. A city bus had struck him as he was riding his bike. There wasn't much the trained emergency responders could do; he was pretty much dead on arrival. Standing with his mother and family, gathered around his body, I experienced the true horror and depth of sorrow. I never found out the cause of the tragedy—whether it was the fault of the bus driver, teen, or some other person. It almost doesn't matter, for all the lives involved were in an instant marked by the teeth of that prowling lion. Evil takes and destroys life.

Evil and the fear that it generates are real forces that we must contend with in life. Ignoring their presence is a strategy most of us employ. The trouble is, of course, that when the lion unexpectedly strikes, our denial leaves us unprepared. Not only does the circumstance rock our world, but it tears at our spirits. How could God let this happen? Why is God so distant? Does God care anymore?

In this chapter, we will take a look at evil and fear. First, we will try to make some theological sense out of these concepts. Where is God when the prowling lion strikes? We will then explore a Jesus story that will give us hope amidst the storms of life. From there, we will imagine what it might look like to resist evil. The value of mercy and an ethic of courage gives us practical ways to respond when faced with adversity. Finally, we will take up the counterintuitive practice of praying for our enemies.

Warning: This chapter is not composed of butterflies and rainbows. We are going on a lion hunt, and it is not for the faint of heart. You might feel uncomfortable along the way as we explore the underside of life. As we crack open the façade of false security, you might even question whether this conversation is necessary. Shouldn't we trust in God's protection against lion attacks and call it a day? Can't we stay wrapped up in the divine bubble wrap of wishful thinking? This naïveté only works until it doesn't.

I am of the opinion that it is better for us to take some courage and face the reality of evil and fear in our world than to pretend that it doesn't exist or won't happen to us. Instead of cowering in fear or living in a deluded bubble, it is better to face the things that threaten life head-on with faith. Trusting in the sure and certain hope that God remains close by and is the source of resurrection, we can find courage. The cross is a symbol of God's triumph in the face of evil and fear. Using the cross as a compass, we can journey where angels fear to go.

A time of significant changes in life offers a golden opportunity for this tough spiritual work. It might even be the case that the event which sparked your transition was itself tragic. When we find ourselves in new situations, reality forces us to adjust our perspectives. Unfamiliar circumstances open hearts and minds in a way that established routines cannot. When the ground is shifting, great is the potential for us to find a new place to stand in our relationship with God and others.

A NOTE TO MY SON:

Dear Noah,

I've given up on bubble wrap as a human protection device. Years ago, I thought that if I could surround you in those air-filled bubbles that we love to pop, you would never get hurt. Life doesn't work like that. As much as I've tried to protect you, you still fell. Knees were cut; they bled or bruised. I also know that your heart broke a time or two along the way.

Life is sometimes hard, unfair, and confusing. Evil and fear are real, and they will invade without much warning.

When bad stuff happens, you will find the challenge at the core of your being. You might even experience a shaken spirit.

Fear not. That is the message the Gospels repeat again and again. Lean into your faith in the Living God, who will never abandon you. Evil is real, but so is God. Trust in God to give you the strength to walk through the fire and storms of life.

Love you always,
Dad

A PRAYER FOR YOU:

Gracious God, the presence of evil in our world presents a formidable foe to our lives. Quickly, we can find ourselves swept up by things that seek to destroy. All too many innocent people have fallen victim to forces beyond their control. Give us the strength to live our lives in hope. Empower us to trust in your presence in the midst of struggle. Deploy us to be bringers of your peace and love to those who are hurting. Through Jesus Christ, amen.

Loving Your Enemies

I used to hate gym class in elementary school. Invariably, the jock-centric gym teachers would pick the "sporty" kids to be captains for the dodgeball teams. Captains would, in turn, choose their friends. One by one. Eventually, this public shaming ritual would get down to the handful of misfits to which I belonged. It was a dreadful experience and a painful memory even today.

Feelings of being unworthy and invaluable are byproducts of dividing and separating people. Experiences that create winners and losers perpetuate divisions and brokenness. Here lies fertile soil for the growth of evil and fear. I'm not melodramatic; a characteristic of teenage school shooters seems to be a deep sense of isolation from their peers.

In the ancient world of the Bible, the division of peoples along ethnic and religious lines was noticeable. Different people separated into different tribes. Wars between sworn enemies were commonplace. Feuds among clans and tribes continued for generations. Hatred for the outsider and the alien festered around many a campfire.

And yet, there was also the reality of living as nomadic peoples in a harsh environment. Survival mandated hospitality to outsiders. You welcomed strangers to your tent. You provided food and shelter to those you met along your travels. Reciprocity was a powerful motivator. You could find yourself in need someday, and your own life could depend upon the kindness of an adversary.

From the experience of wandering in the wilderness comes the Mosaic Law. These holy codes sought to guide all aspects of life, from diet to interpersonal relationships. The most critical expectations were to "love the LORD your God with all your heart, and with all your soul, and with all your might (Deuteronomy 6:5)" and to "love your neighbor as yourself (Leviticus 19:18)." To prevent our tendency to define "neighbor" exclusively in tribal terms, Leviticus explicitly includes the outsider: "The alien who resides with you shall be to you as the citizen among you; you shall love the alien as yourself, for you were aliens in the land of Egypt (Lev. 19:34)."

Centuries later, Jesus clarified any lingering misunderstanding. "You have heard that it was said, 'You shall love your neighbor and hate your enemy.' But I say to you, love your enemies and pray for those who persecute you, so that you may be children of your

Father in heaven; for he makes his sun rise on the evil and on the good, and sends rain on the righteous and on the unrighteous (Matthew 5:43-45)."

Loving enemies and labeling outsiders as neighbors is as counter-cultural today as it was all those centuries ago. Something about it seems to go against conventional wisdom and all common sense. Love is a sentiment reserved for those who love us back. Why would you ever lower your guard and be vulnerable in the face of those who could hurt you or are unknown to you? That's just crazy talk.

And yet, if we never move in the direction of love, we will never move toward peace. Hatred (the active opposite of love) and apathy (its passive but no less destructive cousin) toward the enemy or outsider fertilize the plot where evil and fear grow unchecked. They divide and separate to the point where we no longer see others as human. Eventually, violence is the inevitable outcome.

It's critical for us to give the love of enemies and consideration of the outsider as a neighbor a place in our working theology. God commands us to do as much. When we make the ones who are hard to love into the objects of our compassion, kindness, and understanding, we take a bold step in the direction of God.

A quick note of caution: Loving enemies should not be confused with enduring maltreatment. Physical, sexual, or emotional abuse are *never* acceptable. If someone is harming you or someone you love, you need to take action to stop the violence. Too many people have remained trapped in destructive relationships because they misunderstood Jesus's teachings on loving your enemies. If we find ourselves on a battlefield, we may need to love our enemies at a distance.

Whether done near or far, *loving your enemies* is a refusal to dehumanize another human being. No one, not even someone who does horrible things, should be labeled "unlovable." Likewise, even the purveyor of pure evil ought not to be regarded as lacking the Image of God. God created *all* of humanity and remains in a relationship with *all*.

For us to conceive of someone as being beyond God's love and outside all possibility of forgiveness demonstrates our inability to grasp God's abundant grace. In the game of life, God leaves no one unpicked on the sidelines.

A NOTE TO MY SON:

Dear Noah,

I'm sure you have your list. I have my own. You probably haven't written it down. If you have, destroy it now; it can only get you in trouble if someone happened to discover it. I'm talking about your list of "least favorite" people. You know, the ones you wish would go away. Some might call it a list of "enemies."

These are the people who make life difficult for you. Some might criticize and judge without stopping, while others might be unkind or work against you. It might be a personality thing—like water and oil, you don't mix well with them. In the worst case scenarios, for your health and safety, you need to stay clear of these folks.

Two things. First, it is okay for you to identify your enemies and to be on your guard when you are in their presence. Second, when you interact with them, be sure to let Jesus's love guide your words and actions.

Hate, violence, vengeance, and slander are never appropriate or acceptable options for a Christian. Even if you are locked in a pitched battle against those who are seeking to destroy your very being, you should not return evil for evil. If you do, you will lose your integrity and damage your spirit.

Love alone—as hard as it might be, as impossible to imagine—is the best strategy. Even if you have to do it at a distance, love your enemy and wish them no harm.

Love you always,
Dad

A PRAYER FOR YOU:

Gracious God, sometimes it seems like my enemies are all too strong. When I am scared and frightened, it is tempting to strike first or take any means necessary to destroy them. Give me the courage to take a deep breath and lean into your love. Help me to do what seems impossible: let me love even my enemies. Through Jesus Christ, amen.

The Storm That Made Fishermen Cry

"One day he got into a boat with his disciples, and he said to them, "Let us go across to the other side of the lake." So they put out, and while they were sailing he fell asleep. A windstorm swept down on the lake, and the boat was filling with water, and they were in danger. They went to him and woke him up, shouting, "Master, Master, we are perishing!" And he woke up and rebuked the wind and the raging waves; they ceased, and there was a calm. He said to them, "Where is your faith?" They were afraid and amazed, and said to one another, "Who then is this, that he commands even the winds and the water, and they obey him?"

— Luke 8:22-25

A small group of fishers set off across the lake in a boat. Both the men and the water knew each other. After all, these were the waters that provided their livelihood. Over the years, the fishers and the lake had come to know each other well. They had seen the best and worst each had to offer. As is often the case, respect emerged from experience. Each knew his place in relation to the other.

In the collective experience of ancient mariners and fishers, wind and waves posed a real threat to life. Being caught in a storm—whether on the ocean or the vast inland sea of Galilee—was no small matter. It was so daunting that it shaped their spiritual imagination. Here was the very same chaos that God engaged at the start of creation.

It wasn't until God subdued these raging waters that life had the needed space to flourish. Storm forces remained a constant threat to life. Because a storm could stir up at a moment's notice, they were fearsomely unpredictable—a fact that made them dangerous and resistant to control. A force to be reckoned with, storms served as a good illustration of evil and resultant fear.

When the storm arose on the Sea of Galilee that day, the hearts of the fishers-turned-disciples darkened with fear. It wasn't so much that they were in a storm and taking water into the boat that caused their despair. It was that they were caught up by evil forces beyond their control. They were in the middle of an emergency of faith. Because it was a spiritual crisis, their maritime experience wasn't going to save the day. Only the holy man in their boat could help. It didn't matter that he used to be a "landlubber" carpenter. They knew he had a connection to God, who alone had the power to push back the forces of chaos. The trouble was—he didn't seem to care.

Whenever we find ourselves in a place of chaos and confusion, we are in the same boat, literally, as the disciples were that day. Metaphor and reality collide when we find ourselves unable to handle adverse events as they spiral out of control. Fear is a natural first response. It might help us get to safety. Long term, however, fear leads to dark and destructive places. We can feel alone and like God no longer cares.

Unchecked fear can cause despair to fester in our hearts. When we despair, it can seem like we are out of options, desperate. At this moment, we become dangerous ourselves. Fear can cause us to act in destructive ways. Even the most mild-mannered personality can lash out in uncharacteristic ways and participate in unimaginable violence. We are like a cornered and injured animal—a menace to ourselves and others.

To followers overcome with fear, Jesus demonstrated that God alone has the power to push back the forces of evil. In rebuking the waves, Jesus imitated God's work at the start of creation. After things calmed down, Jesus got to the matter of faith: Where is your faith? Why did you give up your trust in God at the very moment that you needed it most? Why did you allow fear and not faith to guide you?

Breathe. Remember, you are a beloved child of God. Trust that God is not going to leave you alone as chaos and evil swirl about you. You may not have the strength to stop the bad things from happening, but you can hold tightly to God's presence and promise.

Turning to God may not clear the skies instantly. It also doesn't guarantee that our boat won't sink. However, it will help us to get a hold on our fear, preventing us from spiraling out of control within our spirits. Turning to God, we push fear to the side and a clear space appears within us.

Though the storm may rage outside, this inner calm will grant us what is needed to carry onward. We will be able to take a second, deeper breath. Centered in the sure and certain presence of God, we will be better able to marshal all our available strength and wisdom to the task at hand. With fear no longer distracting us or draining our energy, we face the challenge in front of us with our best chance of life.

A NOTE TO MY SON:
Dear Noah,

So, do you remember the day that we were caught out in the storm on Prior Lake? The dark clouds, filled with lightning and thunder, were quickly headed our way and we were out in an aluminum boat in the middle of the water. We headed back, but almost lost the outboard motor in the process. In our rush to shore, I didn't see that the bolts holding the motor to the boat had loosened up. Were it not for my grip on the tiller, the whole outboard would have sunk to the bottom of Prior Lake. That was scary! We were fortunate to make it back to the shore.

As you no doubt already know, life is full of scary storms. Fear is a feeling that is par for the course. When you are afraid, pay close attention. Use fear to make sure that you get to a safe space. However, try not to let fear get out of control. No good ever comes from escalating fear.

Take a deep breath the next time fear comes your way. As you breathe, open your heart, mind, and faith. Trust in

God's presence. You are not alone. There are always options and possibilities.

Love you always,
Dad

A PRAYER FOR YOU:

Gracious God, at the beginning of time, you pushed back the forces of chaos to create life. Be present in the midst of the storms of my life. Push back all fears and form a space wherein I can trust in you. Deliver me from evil so that I might give witness to your love. Through Jesus Christ, amen.

When Evil Loses Its Fangs

Imagine a monster, a hideous, fanged creature with an insatiable appetite for destruction. Does your beast have horns and breathe fire? Did battle scar its visage? Or is your demon easy on the eyes? Maybe your villain teases its victims into lowering their defenses through seduction. What face would you give to evil?

Maybe in your imagination, evil isn't personified. Perhaps it is unseen—a ravenous virus or cancer that tears away from the inside out. Is it found in the impersonal forces of nature, like a hurricane or tornado?

How would you describe your biggest nightmare? What brings you the most fear and keeps you up at night?

After conjuring up in your thoughts that which you are afraid to dream, take a moment of quiet. Breathe. At this time, your nemesis lives only in the space of your imagination. Your thoughts are the only thing keeping it alive right now. As such, you have it captured, and it cannot hurt you. You have an opportunity to examine it. Gaze into its eyes or the center of its being. What do you see?

More importantly, what do you feel? Is it fear or dread? Is it anger and a desire to destroy? What is the source of these feelings? Have you encountered this enemy before? Are your thoughts coming from first-hand experience and suffering? Did something terrible happen to you or someone you love on account of your monster?

Maybe the feelings are coming from a suspicion, bias, or prejudice, or as the result of some propaganda perpetrated by someone who wants you to behave or respond in a certain way. Work your way through how you know that what frightens you is an adversary. What is real and what is fantasy?

After spending some time in the darkness of a worst-case scenario, let's turn toward the light. What would it take to counterbalance your fears? How can you resist the evil that you have identified? How do you keep it at bay without being bitten by its poisonous fangs?

Be careful.

The inclination to destroy evil often does not consider the damage such an action can have on our souls. Violence begets violence; hatred can scar the kindest of hearts. How might the values of love, mercy, and forgiveness be used to resist and disarm your fiendish foe? Think beyond neutralizing your threat: how do you not replace the monster with your own set of fangs?

Now think beyond yourself. How might God rebuke the chaos of your nightmarish storm?
Imagine Jesus walking toward what frightens you. What might Jesus say to the monster to cast it away? What might Jesus tell you that would calm your fears? How

do you feel now? Is there joy or courage to be found in the presence of Jesus?

Where does the power of love come into your story? What strength can you glean from God's grace, forgiveness, and mercy? What kind of miracle would free you from the bondage of your fears and allow you to live boldly?

Do any unexpected possibilities emerge when evil loses its fangs and flees?

Lean enthusiastically into your imagination. Let these dreams push away your nightmares. Breathe in the fresh air, devoid of any monster's putrid breath. Bask in the sunshine of a new day. Wonder what adventures will appear next in your story. Allow anticipatory thanks for God's healing, renewal, and triumph to fill you.

A NOTE TO MY SON:

Dear Noah,

So what's your plan to hold back the forces of evil and all manner of things that go bump in the night? Denial? Pretending that everything is okay? Attacking? Heading right into the struggle with a battle ax swinging? Hiding? Finding a good spot with lots of camouflage and hoping that evil doesn't find you?

All of these strategies are options. Be careful and cautious. Whatever plan you make, be sure that the cure isn't worse than the disease. Be sure not to contribute to evil.

In his hymn, "A Mighty Fortress Is Our God," Martin Luther uses the image of "weapons of the spirit" to talk about the appropriate ways for Christians to resist evil. What might these be?

As I think of it, spiritual weapons include not only prayer but also humility, kindness, mercy, forgiveness, hospitality, and generosity. Such things push away hatred, fear, loneliness, prejudice, and everything that dehumanizes and vilifies others. They disarm suspicion, shatter prejudices, and refuse to escalate further fear.

When heading into spiritual battle, be sure to arm yourself with Jesus's tools and not the devil's. And by all means, leave the bazooka at home!

Love you always,
Dad

A PRAYER FOR YOU:
Gracious God, be with me when I am afraid. In the midst of nightmares real and perceived, calm my troubled spirit with the assurance of your presence. Speak words of love and grace into my ear. Guide me to resist evil without becoming infected by its venom. Let me disarm situations and attacks through the weapons of your spirit. Through Jesus Christ, amen.

Mercy and Forgiveness

It might seem strange to raise the Christian values of mercy and forgiveness in a discussion about evil and fear. After all, don't we need to get tough to battle with the devil and combat terror? Mercy and forgiveness seem all too soft a response; they are too impracticable. Such ideas may be okay in Sunday school, but in the real world, to suggest that they'd work is downright foolish. In the face of hardcore demonic forces, employing mercy and forgiveness seems like using a water gun to fight a forest fire.

Isn't it better for us to arm ourselves with weapons that have actual firepower? We must be aggressive and win at all costs. After all, the one that we've identified as the enemy is less than human and deserves no compassion. We surmise, with self-justifying logic, that they wouldn't show any mercy to us. Therefore, we might even conclude that we need to be preemptive in our strikes because our way is right. At this point, someone will usually mention "god"—a god (of our making) fights by our side and has blessed even the most demonic of our weapons.

Sadly, some version of that story plays out all too often in individual and communal dramas. It is the narrative that pulls at the fabric of families and nations as they do battle. It hardens hearts and clenches fists. It accesses the kind of passions that only escalate and fuel further conflict. Warriors leave their better selves at home as they enthusiastically head toward the battlefield. The cycle of violence, dehumanization, and sin repeats itself once again.

And God weeps from the cross.

Whether on a micro or macro scale, each time a broken creation turns to broken means to solve broken problems, we will get the same result: brokenness. Today's winners will invariably plant seeds of retaliation in the losers' hearts, setting the stage for tomorrow's conflict. The cycles of violence and distrust continue; ultimately, no one wins. Relationships suffer and we cannot form bonds of trust.

There is another way. Jesus offers an alternative to fighting and violence. On the cross, Jesus offered mercy and forgiveness to his executioners. Instead of demanding retribution and revenge, he employed these exceptional values and refused to continue the cycle of violence. Though it is God's right to require justice, God chooses the only thing that will allow for a relationship to continue with humanity: God heads in the direction of mercy.

Mercy occurs whenever we are within our right to punish someone or demand that another pay us back for harming us and we choose not to exercise that right. It is the neighbor who shows compassion and kindness to the neighborhood kid whose baseball breaks a window. It is the judge who sees beyond the facts to understand the circumstances of a crime. Far from weakness, when someone displays mercy, they are exhibiting restraint and control over lustful vengeance.

Forgiveness is similar in both form and function. When you forgive, you look into the face of the one who has hurt you and hold off from taking your pound of flesh. Forgiveness, too, has the effect of breaking the cycle of retaliation. When you withhold your action, there is nothing to counter. Forgiveness puts things to rest; the fire loses its oxygen and can no longer burn.

On a personal level, it can be tough to embrace and apply mercy and forgiveness into our daily routines. In matters both big and small, we want to hang onto the hurt even though it might eat away at us from inside out. We want others to hurt as much as we have and demand they get what's coming to them. I guess it's human nature. But this is the kind of human nature that keeps us restless, in conflict, and at war. Only when we let things go are we able to forge a different relationship with others. In mercy and forgiveness, we find a hope that will ultimately lead to lasting peace.

A NOTE TO MY SON:

Dear Noah,

Sometimes I want to stay mad at people. This is especially true when they have said or done something that has hurt me. There are even times that I want folks who have injured me to suffer themselves.

Whenever I've gone to that dark place, I have discovered that I'm never satisfied. Often, it only makes things worse; for now, mad at me, they want their revenge. It's a bad cycle in which to be found.

Jesus teaches us to be merciful and to forgive others. As hard as this may be, it is the path that leads to a peaceful future. Instead of staying enemies or estranged, when you share these values, you have a chance of making a friend. And if not a friend, then at least one less enemy that wants revenge.

Try it out. Take the harder path. It will help you stay spiritually healthy even in trying and difficult times.

Love you always,
Dad

A PRAYER FOR YOU:

Gracious God, you are merciful, and you forgive me on a daily basis. Although you could hold my shortcomings, poor decisions, and mistakes against me, you don't. Instead, you refuse to let my sins get in the way of your love. Let me imitate your mercy and forgiveness in my dealings with others. Through my words and actions, turn me away from the cycles of vengeance and violence. Guide my feet on the path of peace. Through Jesus Christ, amen.

Seeking Peace

On the shelf in my church study, there is a broken chalice. This sacramental cup didn't start out in pieces. It was a present from my wife, Katie, on the one-year anniversary of my ordination. She had someone in my internship congregation throw it on her potter's wheel. For years, I used it on retreats, as it was the perfect size for small-group eucharistic celebrations. Carefully, I carted it all over the place. On the move from New Jersey to Minnesota, I wrapped it in large bubble wrap to protect it. I had it proudly displayed in my new pastor's study at the church in Burnsville.

Everything was fine with the vessel until one day, someone knocked it over. That was all it took to crack and eventually break apart into shards of varying sizes. When the shock wore off, I was angry. I judged the person to be careless. Although it was purely an accident, I interpreted the incident in the worst of ways. The breaking of my chalice added tension and hurt feelings to a relationship that was already strained and frayed. As the "injured party," I allowed the situation to contribute fuel to a festering fire.

Looking back, I'm not proud of my response. In a classic passive-aggressive fashion, I never confronted the one who broke my cup. When it fell over, it didn't shatter at first. I picked it up and reset it on the table. Only when the person left my study did I investigate further. That was when I discovered the breakage. But I kept silent and never shared my hurt. Whenever I passed the busted cup on my shelf, I judged that "scoundrel" anew and kept the wound open in my heart.

In the face of brokenness, how does a Christian respond? What ethics can guide both our thoughts and actions?

How do we relate to those who have hurt us or who wish us ill?

We have already talked about the importance of the values of mercy and forgiveness. These Jesus-centric values invite us to turn from our inward, passive-aggressive places to engage with others positively. Jesus calls us to the hard work of love. Instead of barricading ourselves in self-righteous towers, ready for war, the values of mercy and forgiveness turn in the outward direction of peace.

James M. Childs, Jr., a Lutheran ethicist, writes:

> Peace does not come cheaply when parties are in conflict and wrongs have been done. The process of reconciliation is not one of papering over the hurts and the wrongs with a too-easy forgiveness. Neither is it a matter of overlooking those wrongs and allowing them to go unchallenged. Rather, reconciliation requires acknowledging wrongs, repentance, and a commitment to change. This will often involve confronting persons in the role they have played in creating a situation of conflict or estrangement.[2]

---

[2] James M. Childs, *Faith, Formation, and Decision; Ethics in the Community of Promise* (Philadelphia: Fortress Press, 1992),69-70.

Seeking peace is not avoiding conflict and being "Minnesota nice." It is turning toward an adversary and seeing them as a brother or sister. When you desire peace, you refuse to let the past prevent the future.

The concept of peace—in Hebrew, *shalom*—is not to be understood merely as an absence of conflict. It is much more. *Shalom* is wholeness. Things are where they should be in relation to one another. Not only can you see the restoration and reconciliation, you can feel it in every cell of your being.

You don't get to this place by ignoring hurts or engaging in passive-aggressive behavior. You also don't win peace by dominating your opponent and beating them into submission. *Shalom* comes only through the acknowledgment of the other as an equal in the sight of God. It comes through empathetic engagement of their needs and fears.

Again, it's not easy work by any means. Ironically, in some ways, fighting a war is the path of least resistance. It doesn't take much care to hurl a flaming cocktail, whether it be metaphorical or literal. Conflicts, however, have a way of spinning out of control. Consider the damage that a single uncaring social media post can do. Unchecked, each little post, each small action will eventually lead to violence and the suffering of the innocent. In a world where our bombs are bigger and more destructive than ever, the stakes are high.

So what makes for peace? For starters, it is good to ask this very question. Consider first, instead of just reacting—whether aggressively or passively. As we relate to others, friends and enemies alike, what makes for peace? What words and actions might we take in love toward another? I know a first-grade teacher who would always remind her kids to make "loving choices." What might we say and do that is rooted in love?

When we are active in love, we assume the role of peacemaker. No matter the size, each loving contribution that we make each day has the potential of accumulating into something bigger. Bit by bit, we lean into the incoming kingdom of God. Incrementally, we creep in the direction of *shalom*. Even when we take steps backward—we remain imperfect and broken beings, after all—there will be a net gain over time as we seek peace.

I keep the broken chalice on a shelf in my pastor's study. Though I can no longer use it for eucharistic celebration, it continues to serve a useful purpose. It reminds me on a daily basis of the brokenness of life and of my call to be a peacemaker.

A NOTE TO MY SON:
Dear Noah,

Each day of school, you are one day closer to graduation. It may not seem like it, especially as you become swamped with work, study, and the need to get enough sleep. But you are on a path that leads somewhere.

Life is like that—it is a journey full of unexpected twists, challenges, joys, and sorrows. Even if it turns out that graduation doesn't happen, you will have acquired experience from your time at school.

Each day we take a step into our future. The question that we must ask ourselves is: Are we making these steps in love? Are we choosing peace? Instead of working against others, either actively or passively, do we work for them? In all relationships, do we embody generosity, kindness, compassion, humility, etc.? Do we try to act like Jesus?

I will let you ponder these questions as you walk about on campus.

Love you always,
Dad

By the way, I was just raising the hypothetical scenario of not graduating. Your future will be so much brighter with that piece of paper hanging on your wall along the way. So hang in there—it is worth it!

A PRAYER FOR YOU:

Gracious God, you said, "blessed are the peacemakers." Guide me this day on the way to peace. Direct my words and deeds to be compassionate, kind, generous, and caring. Help me to connect with others in such a manner that builds relationships that reflect your love. Through Jesus Christ, amen.

Praying for Your Enemies

Years ago, during the first Iraq War, a few pastors got in trouble for praying for Saddam Hussein. That's un-American! Unless you are praying for his destruction and demise, you can't pray for the enemy. During a time of war, doing so seems like you are praying against your nation and its soldiers!

I wasn't one of those pastors; I couldn't do it. It was beyond my holy imagination and general sensibility to pray for the one who had invaded another nation and attacked civilian populations. At that time, Jesus's words to love your enemies did not find a place within my heart.

Throughout this chapter, we have focused on how we can face evil and fear in our lives. We have considered both real and imaginary threats to our safety and spirits. At various points, we examined the subject of enemies. We all have those folks in our lives who always seem to contradict our efforts, ideas, and existence. We may not label these adversaries "enemies" as such, because that sounds so harsh. Still, they are not friends, and we are not generally accustomed to wishing them well. We may not pray *against* them, but we are not rushing to put them on our prayer list.

But what if we did? What would it be like to pray for the very last person who comes to our mind? If Jesus's command to love our enemies is to be given credence, then maybe saying a little prayer for these folks isn't the worst idea. Let's try it out.

Take a deep breath. Quiet your spirit and clear your mind. After you are in a non-anxious space, think of someone who has hurt or harmed you. Perhaps it was a careless word or thoughtless action. Maybe it is your nemesis, who always seems to take away your joy or foil your plans. It may be that you don't even know their name, but they cut you off on the road and you are mad at them. For whatever reason, this person might be hard for you to love.

Picture their face, complete with its insincere smile or sinister glare. Don't clean up your emotions. Don't shut the door to anger or resentment. Keep your prayer real.

Turn to God. Invite God's presence into the uncomfortable and troubled space of your heart. Resist the urge to ask God to change them. The goal is not to summon divine agency to disarm another or to join our side in our struggle. Simply pray *for* them. Pray for *them*. Ask God to bless their spirit with the love of Jesus.

Conclude by asking God to give you the courage and strength to love your enemies. Let the words be few and allow your prayer to linger in silence.

How did it feel? Was it weird and unsettling, a strange thing to do? Did it feel wrong? Why might that have been?

Or did this exercise have a surprising effect? Did it help you to see someone else in a different light? Did your prayer create a tiny space of understanding? Perhaps you caught a glimpse of humanity in someone you labeled as a demon.

No matter how it felt the first time, try it again. Pray again for your enemies in the same tone that you reserve for honored friends. Allow God to use your prayer to work something new in your heart. Push away any feelings of hate. Lean into God's mercy and grace to plant the seeds of forgiveness and peace.

Prayer offers a safe place for us to address our enemies. Maybe it is the only place where you can approach an adversary without risking further harm. Use it and let it transform the scars and hardness of your spirit. Trust that when you are in prayer, God is near—you don't have to worry about defending or protecting yourself.

Instead, let God control the divided ground between you and your enemy, turning it into a sacred space where healing and transformation can happen. Seek the peace that occurs through reconciliation and restoration. Yearn for a time when neither of you clenches your fists but instead can hold hands. Impossible? Inconceivable? Impracticable?

In prayer, we turn to God, through whom all things are possible. Ultimately God will renew all things, even Middle East dictators and followers of Jesus with limited imaginations.

A NOTE TO MY SON:

Dear Noah,

Okay, here is your crazy father once again with a strange idea. Think of a person that you don't like. Maybe they aren't the nicest to you. At the start of each day for a week, I want you to pray for them. It doesn't need to be anything fancy or complicated. A simple, single-sentence prayer will do: Dear God, bless [insert name here] today and give me the strength to love them.

See what happens. Does your praying have any effect on your heart or on the way that you perceive this person? Does it help you to understand them better or push aside any resentment that you might hold against them?

Prayer is a powerful balm for wounded spirits. When we connect with God, who is the source of all healing, it has a positive effect not only on us but also on our relationships with others. Pray often and pray from your heart.

Love you always,
Dad

A PRAYER FOR YOU:

Gracious God, Jesus commanded me to love my enemies. I have a hard time with this. It seems so strange and counterintuitive to even pray for some folks. Guide my prayer so that it might have a place for those I'd rather leave out. Open my heart toward those I do not like and have a hard time loving. Replace my feelings of anger and hate with your compassion and love. Through Jesus Christ, amen.

CHAPTER FIVE

WON'T YOU BE MY NEIGHBOR?

I will not deny it, I'm a big fan of Fred Rodgers. Some of my earliest TV memories consist of watching *Mr. Rodgers' Neighborhood*. Although I didn't know it at the time, Fred Rodgers was a Presbyterian minister. From an electronic pulpit, Rodgers preached a doctrine of loving the neighbor in such a way that delighted and instructed children for decades (1968–2000).

Watching this kind and gentle spirit interact with all the different people in his never-ending neighborhood, my concept of neighbor was expanded. Everyone, no matter where they lived, could be considered a neighbor, not just those who lived literally next door.

It might seem strange to think about our neighbors in a book that looks at navigating life's transitions. Shouldn't we be focusing more on ourselves? We know that everyone, all around us, is struggling with their unique problems, worries, and challenges. Instead of burdening others or taking on more ourselves, shouldn't we let everyone take care of themselves? I'll concern myself with my changes, and I'll leave you to yours. No sense in adding to one's struggles.

The problem with such thinking is that it increases isolation and contributes to division among folks. All too often, we face hardship alone. Perhaps we don't want to overload others with a burden of care. Or we may not think that they could comprehend what we are facing. And so, we choose to encounter change and uncertainty by ourselves. Contrary to our created nature—God created us to live in community, after all—we opt to live, as Thoreau once said, "lives of quiet desperation." Silently, we suffer and muddle through.

There is an alternative. At the moment when life seems to be out of our control, instead of turning inward, we can choose to open our eyes and hearts toward our neighbors, those whom we live near and interact with on a daily basis.

These folks include members of our tribe and clan, with whom we share a blood relationship. We know who these folks are and we share with them the common bonds of belief, history, proximity, and familiarity. That is the narrowest circle that scripture draws to define neighbor. A strict interpretation of the commandment to love thy neighbor, therefore, means to love those who are part of our inner circle.

Lest we focus our definitions too stringently, the divine admonition to consider the alien as a neighbor and then to love that neighbor as you do yourself suggests a need to widen the circle (Leviticus 19:34.) Jesus challenges the scribes and the Pharisees on this very point. In sharing table fellowship with outsiders and telling stories about helpful Samaritans, Jesus significantly broadens the concept of neighbor.

In this chapter, I will suggest that focusing on neighbors is not only the right thing to do but is also beneficial to our spirits. That is true even when we face uncertainty and changing landscapes. We will ground neighborly conversation in the theological concept of *Imago Dei.* This idea can influence our working theology in powerful ways. Our Jesus story will be a familiar tale about a courageous individual who stepped outside his neighborhood and redefined what it means to be a good neighbor. We will imagine hosting a large dinner party with a bunch of unusual guests. From there, we will look at the value of inclusion and an ethic of hospitality.

Finally, our prayer practice will involve sending notes of appreciation.

Before we head out into the neighborhood, let's change into our "outside" shoes. Put on your cardigan sweaters and sing a few bars of "Won't You Be My Neighbor."

A NOTE TO MY SON:
Dear Noah,

Do you know your neighbors yet? You know, the people who live in the rooms adjacent to yours in the dorm. How about the people who live on the same floor? How about the building? So many people live within close proximity that it will be almost impossible for you to know all your neighbors.

Oh, I'm sure you'll get to know the names, faces, and behaviors of your closest neighbors. For better or worse. Some will be good. Others will drive you crazy. No matter; take a deep breath and remember that God wants you to love them all. Show each the honor and respect that you would like them to show you. When they don't, keep at it.

Keeping widening your understanding of both who your neighbor is and the boundaries of your neighborhood.

Love you always,
Dad

A PRAYER FOR YOU:
Gracious God, you call us to love our neighbors as we love ourselves. Give me the wisdom and strength to follow your command. Help me to be a good neighbor in all the places that I find myself. Through Jesus Christ, amen.

Imago Dei

"So God created humankind in his image, in the image of God he created them."

—Genesis 1:27a

As we build our working theology, one of the most useful ideas for us to consider is the concept of *Imago Dei*. It comes from the first chapter of Genesis and has a history of use in Christianity and Judaism. What this idea, translated as the "image of God," means is open for interpretation: Is this the Divine Spark? Is it a necessary ingredient in the atoning fight against original sin? Or is it merely a reminder that there is something of God in each human being?

Back in the early 2000s, as I was working on and studying the sermons of Archbishop Desmond Tutu, I was forever changed by his use of *Imago Dei*. For him, the concept was central to his Ubuntu theology. If God created every human being in God's image, then each ought to be treated with reverence and respect. Racism and division among people are ungodly and work against the created order.

Those who perpetuate ideas of racial or ethnic superiority deny God's image and are committing blasphemy of the highest order. One need not look any further than Genesis 1:27 to see that Apartheid in South Africa and Jim Crow in America were morally wrong. No matter how stridently white churches tried to defend these practices using scripture (and they did for some time), it doesn't hold up to the simple truth of *Imago Dei*.

On a personal level, I have found *Imago Dei* to be a handy idea. It means that God is present in everyone I meet. God is present in those who look like me, think like me, and share my affinity for anchovies. *And*, perhaps more importantly, God is present in those who don't look like me, think like me, or eat salty fish. Underneath and underlying all the diversity, difference, and division, I share a common identity with every living human being on the planet. From innocent babies to convicted felons, there is something of God in each of us. We are all children of God. No exceptions.

As is often the case, applying a principle can be hard to do. I continue to find myself wanting there to be an exception or loophole. It can be hard to look in the face of someone who is violently opposed to your very being and spurting vile criticisms and say that God created them in God's image. But even these people are part of the *all*. I have found myself challenged to open the hardest places of my heart. If I can't demonize or dehumanize my neighbor, then I need to find ways to love them. Yes, even *them*!

I'm not always successful in my efforts. Biases and prejudices continue to fester in hidden places of my heart that prevent me from fully embracing this idea. I remain in need of continual repentance and forgiveness. In those moments, I am glad that *Imago Dei* also applies to me. Even though I'm not fully able to embrace God's presence in everyone, it remains in them and *me*! I am unable to escape being made in God's image. Since God remains in me, there is hope. Hope, still, that I will lean into this identity as I engage my neighbor.

A NOTE TO MY SON:

Dear Noah,

Two things will always be true. One: you are a child of God. Two: so is everybody else!
Why is this important? I have found that I get myself into trouble when I forget these two things. When I forget that God created me and everybody else in God's image, I either think too highly or too lowly of myself and others. This is not good.

A helpful hint to correct this vision problem involves a mirror. When you look in the mirror each morning, say to yourself: I am a child of God, created in God's image. Then repeat the phrase "child of God, created in God's image" to the very next face you see, whether in person or on TV or on your phone. It will help to change the way you see yourself and others.

Love you always,
Dad

A PRAYER FOR YOU:

Gracious God, you created all humanity in your image. Help me to claim this identity for myself and others. Guide my words and actions so that I might live out this truth in this day. Through Jesus Christ, amen.

To Be or Not To Be a Neighbor ?

"But a Samaritan while traveling came near him; and when he saw him, he was moved with pity. He went to him and bandaged his wounds, having poured oil and wine on them. Then he put him on his own animal, brought him to an inn, and took care of him. The next day he took out two denarii, gave them to the innkeeper, and said, "Take care of him; and when I come back, I will repay you whatever more you spend." Which of these three, do you think, was a neighbor to the man who fell into the hands of the robbers? He said, "The one who showed him mercy." Jesus said to him, "Go and do likewise."

— Luke 10:33-37

The tale of the Good Samaritan is one of the most memorable and repeated of all Jesus's stories. It's a great story with all the essential elements. There is drama, suspense, villains, hero, and a human need that cries out. We tell this story to our kids to encourage within them a desire to help others: be like the Samaritan who showed selfless compassion.

We should also tell this story to our kids to teach them about neighbors.

After all, Jesus initially told this story in response to a question about who we should consider to be our neighbor. An educated man, one who studied and knew his Bible, asked because he wanted to get it right.

As I mentioned at the start of this chapter, "neighbor" can be defined in various ways. A strict definition would include only those who are of the same blood, tribe, proximity, and belief system. Neighbors share a similar status, demographics, and economic conditions. Those outside this group do not fall under the commandment's directive to love.

Outsiders are a potential threat and caution should be exercised when dealing with them. Only in the case where an alien resides in your midst do you have to consider them a neighbor. Although this provision opens the door to thinking more broadly about neighbors, it still limits the concept to your location. Neighbors live only in your neighborhood. At least, that was the conventional wisdom at the time of Jesus's earthly ministry.

Was it something in the way that Jesus was teaching or sharing table fellowship with outsiders that prompted the lawyer to ask his question about the neighbor? Why did he need to justify himself? Was it because that Jesus seemed to apply a different definition of neighbor in his public ministry?

In any case, at the end of the story, Jesus asks the lawyer to draw a conclusion about who acted like a neighbor. Of course, it was the Samaritan! Go and do likewise!

But here is the catch. To go and consider a Samaritan a neighbor would be to disregard centuries of isolation and separation between Jews and Samaritans. Though in the far past a relationship existed, history tore them apart and kept them at a distance. In no recent calculation were these groups considered neighbors.

Since they weren't technically "neighbors," God's commands to love them didn't apply.

At least, not according to the conventional wisdom in which the lawyer was schooled. If he was going to follow Jesus's understanding of living in a right relationship with God, then he was going to have to broaden his imagination. He was going to need to relabel those he previously designated as outsiders. Which, of course, meant that he was going to need to start loving a whole lot more.

Could that be the whole point of the story? We are not only asked to show compassion to those in need; what Jesus really wants is for us to widen our thoughts about who we consider to be our neighbor. In the next section, we will spend some time imagining what this might mean. For now, let's focus on the need to move the boundary of who is our neighbor.

Whether or not the place where we live has literal fences, there is always a boundary around neighborhoods. Instinctively, we know whether someone is "from around here" or not. We know because buried deep within us are boundary markers. Social conditioning and traditions etched these markers into our hearts over the course of years.

By looking into the face of another, we instantly know if they are one of our "peeps." As soon as we make such an observation, we usually make a judgment about that person. This judgment, in turn, will determine our response to them. In a split second, we will either be a neighbor or something else.

What if between recognition and judgment we inserted a holy pause?

In Jesus's story, had the priest or the Levite—both presumably good people—had taken a moment in their quick walk past their fellow human, hurt on the side of the road, things might have been different. I think the reason they didn't stop was that they didn't recognize the injured man as their neighbor, and therefore they quickly judged that this wasn't their problem.

Surely, if they acknowledged the man as a neighbor, they would have stopped, if only to follow God's commands. Had they paused for the briefest of moments and looked through the holy lens of Jesus, they would have seen what the Samaritan saw. They would have seen the person in need as a neighbor. And that sight alone would have compelled them to be a neighbor in return.

What would it mean to us if we went and did likewise?

A NOTE TO MY SON:

Dear Noah,

When you look at someone else—stop! Before you make any judgments about where they might be from and what they might know, think of them first as your neighbor.

Don't get me wrong: if they are coming at you swinging an ax, get out of the way. You can label that person an "enemy" and take evasive action. For all others, however, give them the benefit of the doubt and start with "neighbor."

Why is this important? Try it out and get back to me.

Love you always,
Dad

A PRAYER FOR YOU:

Gracious God, give me the vision of the Samaritan that allowed him to see the one in need as a neighbor. Draw me into a compassionate response when I encounter familiar and unfamiliar faces alike. Through Jesus Christ, amen.

You Are about To Host a *Big* Party

Though she didn't have any professional food-service training, my mother knew how to host a big party. When I was in high school, about three times a year, my parents hosted dinner for thirty to forty people. These grand banquets required us to clear out the furniture in the living room to make space for the tables that we borrowed from our church.

Mom did all the cooking, making sauerbraten and corned beef with cabbage for the masses. Dad took care of stocking and chilling the beverages. In addition to feasting, there was singing and dancing. Lots of laughter filled the house.

The regularity of these events prompted guests to ask about the date of the next one so that they could get it on the calendar. Over time, the eclectic group of family, friends, and guests got to know one another. As a result of my parents' hospitality, friendships emerged around the borrowed banquet tables. Over time, strangers became neighbors, part of the Lichtenberger family.

Imagine you are going to host a big gathering. Don't worry about the food or if you have enough space. Think about the people. Who would you invite? What names and faces pop into your mind immediately? Are they blood relations or close friends? Extended family?

At first, think only about those you want to be at your party. Who are those people who make you smile and laugh, whom you are always happy to see? So far, I'm guessing this whole exercise has been pleasurable. Who doesn't want to be around people who bring joy, happiness, and friendship to life?

Even if your initial list is massive, more in number than you have room to host, continue to imagine. It is time to add more guests. Think of folks who live in your neighborhood. Invite the ones you know by name and the ones you know only by sight. How about the person you wave to as they jog or walk their dog by your house? These are all your neighbors by the strictest of definitions. Ask them to come by so that you can get to know them and start to love them.

Continue with the list. Now include the ones about whom you don't usually think. By definition, this will be harder because you don't often consider these folks. They fade into the background of your busy life. Some hide in plain sight, like the person begging on the corner with a cardboard sign. Others cower in the shadows, like the migrant who lacks the proper papers or the abused mother who doesn't want anyone to notice her bruises. How about the stoned drug user who is tripping out? Do you have space in your heart for them? What would it take to love each of these also as your neighbor?

Think now of the very last person you would like to come to your party. Who is your nemesis in life—that person who works tirelessly to get you down? Add that person and any associated villainous characters to your list.

Look over your list. How big and unrealistic did it become? Who are the most unlikely guests? Ask yourself why? Be honest. What is preventing you from inviting them to your party? Is it fear? Prejudice?

Wariness of the social retribution you will suffer from asking the wrong folks? Or is it merely that it is awkward to approach strangers?

Now, wonder about the feast that Isaiah describes: "On this mountain, the LORD of hosts will make for all peoples a feast of rich food, a feast of well-aged wines, of rich food filled with marrow, of well-aged wines strained clear (Isaiah 25:6-7)." It will be the grandest of all parties. What is more, everyone—absolutely *everyone*—is on the guest list.

From the top of your hypothetical invite list to the absolute bottom, all will be there. God will lower all the boundaries and heal all the divisions at the great feast. Old bonds will strengthen. New friendships will form. It will be a glorious day that inaugurates a community in which all live as neighbors. On that day, love will be both the language and system of exchange. Not a single person will be left out.

It is the kind of dream that is worth our time and imagination. It is a destination toward which each of us would do well to travel. It is a hope that should inspire us the next time we make up an invite list.

A NOTE TO MY SON:

Dear Noah,

What is the biggest room on campus? Picture it filled with tables and chairs—hundreds of them. Imagine a feast filled with all the very best foods, all of your favorites. It's your party, so you can invite anyone you would like.

Who would be on your guest list? I'm sure you'd invite your friends and family (don't forget your dad!). Perhaps acquaintances and maybe even your teachers would also get an invite.

Now imagine that there is still room. Who else would you let come? Would you grab unknown students and their friends? Would you go out into the streets and bring in complete strangers? How far would you go to invite people?

Hard to picture, isn't it? But difficult as it is even to imagine, that is what is on God's mind when it comes to the heavenly feast. Everyone at the table. Let that image inspire you the next time you head into the cafeteria.

Love you always,
Dad

A PRAYER FOR YOU:

Gracious God, great is your steadfast love for all humanity, and your hospitality exceeds our imagination. Inspire us as we set our tables to reflect your gracious invitation. Open our hearts so that they might have space for all. Through Christ, amen.

Inclusion

It was a tremendous experience to be one of 35,000 participants at the ELCA Youth Gathering in Houston. Throughout four days of mass gatherings, we heard a variety of voices as speakers shared both their struggles and their faith. Each contributed a unique perspective to the gathering's theme of "This Changes Everything," encouraging us to be part of a church in which everyone has a place.

For me, unquestionably, the best witness came from a little eleven-year-old girl, who was introduced by her mother. Her smile captivated the Super Bowl-sized NRG stadium. Rebekah Bruesehoff spoke with passion and clarity about the welcome she received from her parents, her church, and her God. Rebekah is transgender. Rebekah; her mom, Jamie; and her off-stage, pastor dad, Chris, all embody the critical Gospel-centric value of inclusion.

I am proud to serve as a pastor in a national church body that dares to embrace inclusion. Inviting an articulate transgender pre-teen to speak at a youth gathering was a bold move that no doubt ruffled some feathers. Though I didn't see it in the section where I was sitting, I'm told by colleagues that some adult leaders removed their groups from the arena before Rebekah and Jamie spoke. Although they received a heartfelt standing ovation from the crowd when they finished, I'm sure that not everyone was happy with what they experienced.

I must admit that the whole idea of transgender forces one to rethink traditional categories of the created order. Whereas I don't pretend to understand the reality of being transgendered or of having a transgendered child, I don't need to fully "get it" to include those who are in my definition of neighbor and church family.

When Rebekah and Jamie stood on that stage, they didn't ask for my or anyone's approval. They shared their story as a way to open hearts and minds so that there might be a greater space within the church for others with similar experiences.

They stood with courage, willing to be vulnerable for the sake of introducing themselves as God made them. No pretensions. Children of God, who also happen to be a pre-teen transgendered youth and her mother. Children of God, who found a space of welcome in their Christian community. Children of God, who seek inclusion in the larger body of Christ without having first to deny themselves.

The value of inclusion is not some left-wing, secular conspiracy; rather, it is grounded firmly in scripture. Let me share a few instances. When Isaiah dreams of God preparing a mountaintop banquet, he sees *all people* feasting together (Isaiah 25:6). Throughout Jesus's ministry, he was continually sharing table fellowship with a diverse group of people that included self-righteous Pharisees, tax collectors, women with sullied reputations, those with physical impediments, children, and an assorted group of "unclean" characters (see Luke 5:27-39; 7:36-50;9:10-17; 14:1-6, 7-14,15-24; 19:1-10.)

Table fellowship in the Roman world conveyed with it a sort of acceptance, honor, and equal standing. When you ate with someone, you befriended them and entered into a relationship with them. Continued sharing of table fellowship solidified and strengthened social, economic, and religious bonds.

Because of this, folks heavily guarded admittance to the table. You didn't haphazardly eat with just anyone. On more than one occasion, the Pharisees reminded Jesus of the social conventions and implications of his presence at unsavory tables and his open practices of inclusive hospitality.

I'm convinced that Jesus didn't need this "helpful advice," for he thoroughly knew what he was doing. In sharing meals and welcome with those whom society generally excluded, Jesus created a new community that has a place for everyone. Inclusion was a Jesus-value, one established centuries before any current political ideology or secular predisposition.

When the ELCA welcomed Rebekah and Jamie to the stage, the church was living out the same value of inclusion that Jesus displayed time and again when he shared an open table fellowship.

How might we do the same? How can we engage in genuine acceptance of others who may not think, act, or orient themselves as we do? What will it take for us to withhold judgment and instead extend kindness? Personally, what is getting in your way of mimicking Jesus's inclusive table fellowship? How might we follow the courageous witness of an eleven-year-old transgendered girl who was willing to be vulnerable and stood on a stage to share her beautiful smile?

A NOTE TO MY SON:
Dear Noah,

I was happy to see a lot of posters on your campus embracing the value of inclusion. I'm glad that in some places, the acceptance of differences and embracing of diversity is being held up as a goal. Not everything about our culture is terrible.

When multiple orientations, divergent identities, and various self-expressions are displayed out in the open, it will threaten some folks. They will judge. Some might even respond with harmful and hurtful words and actions.

Don't let a lack of understanding turn you away from following Jesus's path of love. Instead, use the occasion of difference as an opportunity to broaden your mind and heart. Don't ever be afraid that you will lose yourself by listening to the experience of another. You only stand to gain from a broader perspective.

Remember, inclusion is never a bad word—it is a Jesus-word.

Love you always,
Dad

A PRAYER FOR YOU:

Gracious God, though you have created all people in your image, we are not the same. There is so much diversity that at times it is hard to comprehend it all. Give me the wisdom to see the blessing in the difference of others. Open my heart and mind so that I can be present in such a way that I can honor and respect even those I cannot fully understand. Through Jesus Christ, amen.

Hospitality

Jesus's passion to show hospitality toward the outsider is critical. It was a driving ethic in his ministry and pushed him to extend his table fellowship and friendship to those who were on the fringes of the neighborhood.

It is important to note that Jesus's understanding of hospitality differs from how we might commonly think of it these days. It is not merely what we share with our friends when they come to dinner or the coffee that we serve in the fellowship hall at church to the usual crowd on a Sunday morning. It is not exclusively the product of a lucrative industry of food and drinks to those who can afford to pay the concierge. Jesus's hospitality focuses on those who are unable to reciprocate.

Jesus's ethic of hospitality extends to those who Christine Pohl describes as *people without a place*:

> Strangers are "people without a place." To be without a place means to be detached from basic, life-supporting institutions—family, work, polity, religious community—and to be without networks of relations that sustain and support human beings. People without a place who are also

without financial resources are the most vulnerable people.[3]

Those *without place* and networks of support are to be the primary recipients of hospitality if we are to follow in the table manners and ethics of Jesus. But how do we do this? How do we extend hospitality with the context of a suburban community where there is isolation between neighbors and carefully constructed gates (some of which are invisible) keeping those without out of our sight?

These are real and tough questions. It becomes even more challenging when we face transitions and changes. How do we extend hospitality to outsiders when we have circled our proverbial wagons in fear or we are uncertain what the future might bring?

The first step along the journey involves understanding that we are the recipients of God's gracious hospitality. We, who have become strangers in our sin and brokenness, receive God's welcome. Pohl writes, "A life of hospitality begins in worship, with a recognition of God's grace and generosity. Hospitality is not first a duty and

---

[3] Christine D. Pohl. *Making Room: Recovering Hospitality as a Christian Tradition*, (Grand Rapids:W.B. Eerdmans Publishing, 1999), 87.

responsibility; it is first a response of love and gratitude for God's love and welcome to us."[4]

Experiencing God's hospitality within worship is a critical first step, but truly embracing God's hospitality involves participating in it for the restoration of those outside the church. God's hospitality does not limit itself to any one community but always pushes outward. Ultimately, the goal is to exchange hospitality with those on the fringes, with *people without a place.* We need to take more small steps to head in this direction.

Paying attention to the strangers in our midst, and looking for the Christ in them, allows us to claim a servant identity that is crucial to the life of discipleship. Small gestures—a smile or some other expression of kindness—are a big deal. The sharing of food and drink without expectation of reciprocity is another step. Taking the time to listen is another still.

Whenever we share our time, our attention, or our resources with another, we engage in hospitality. Generosity and kindness accompany acts of genuine hospitality. When we give without expectation,

---

[4] Ibid, 172.

something remarkable happens: we also receive blessings. Mutual benefits emerge in the practice of hospitality.

The ethical practice of hospitality is ultimately an act of transformation in which strangers become friends, the placeless find places, aliens become residents, empty lives become filled with blessings, scarcity gives way to abundance, hurts become healed, and lives (our own included) are forever changed.

A NOTE TO MY SON:
Dear Noah,

How's your hospitality these days? Have you been sharing with others?

As a college student, you may not have a lot of stuff, money, or even time. You might think, "someday I'll be better able to give." When you make your first zillion dollars (I'm exaggerating here) or when you have twelve weeks of vacation (exaggerating again) or when you settle down into your castle with an alligator-filled moat (hey, it might be possible), then, you'll be in a place where you can make a difference.

My experience with generosity is that it has less to do with what you have in your hands than it does with what you have in your heart. Some of the most generous and hospitable people I know are the ones without much in the way of earthly treasures. They give from their essence and not from their abundance. And they are generally happy.

In contrast is the miser who is perpetually frightened that he is going to lose his stash. Holding tight to what he has hoarded, he lacks true contentment. He lives in scarcity and will never have enough.

Don't wait to start giving and sharing what you have with others. There is no perfect time to begin to be hospitable except right now!

Love you always,
Dad

A PRAYER FOR YOU:

Gracious God, you are beyond generous with me. Your love and grace rain upon me in buckets. Because of your hospitality, I have a place in you. Make me aware of this gift so that I might emulate your movements. Strengthen me in my sharing of kindness and generosity with others. Move me beyond me to those without a place, who are in desperate need of welcome. Let your hospitality become a way of life for me. Through Jesus Christ, amen.

Praying with a Pen

In the age of instant communication, there is something special about handwritten notes. To receive one in the mail is a gift. Someone took the time to write down their thoughts, which usually convey some gratitude or feeling of concern.

Though some might dismiss handwritten notes as tokens of nostalgic sentimentality, writing notes is an invigorating practice that I have incorporated into my ministry. I have set writing cards of appreciation as one of my weekly lead measures.

I first learned of the concept of "lead measures" through reading the work of management guru Steven Covey. Covey advocates identifying and then measuring those activities that contribute to the accomplishment of a goal (see Steven Covey, *Predictable Results in Unpredictable Times*). Lead measures look to the future and take positive steps toward making a difference in what is to come. If, as I did, you want to nurture relationships in ministry, then connecting with folks by sending notes of appreciation works toward that goal.

What I discovered by sending my notes of appreciation out each week was that I couldn't help but give thanks to God in the process. Along with each card I wrote, a prayer followed. I found myself praying while I was writing. My lead measure effort to nurture relationships with those who I have the privilege of serving as pastor turned into a prayer practice.

Try it out. Perhaps you already have a few blank thank-you cards in your desk. Get one out and take a deep breath. Think about someone who has touched your life. Who has demonstrated to you the love and grace of God?

In your mind's eye, see their face. Share a quick thought of gratitude to God for them and get writing. Let your pen dance upon the page as your heart connects with the writing surface. Tell them how much they mean to you or how thankful you are for them in your life. You can even mention that you have said a prayer of thanks to God for them. When you finish, seal the envelope literally with an *amen.*

You can modify this prayer practice. Instead of sharing words of appreciation, you might want to go the route of intercession. Let them know that you are praying for their healing or strength as they go through a difficult time.

What if, instead of writing to family and friends, you sent a note to a neighbor? Maybe someone you haven't seen in a while but ran into at the supermarket? What would it be like to write a note to the local firehouse or police station thanking them for their service? Be creative.

Try the practice out for a week. Each day, pray for another person as you write to them. Send out the cards with the confidence that God will use your effort to bless another. For, in a few days, when the recipients are sorting through a stack of bills, political ads, and promotional trash, they will find your note. It will unexpectedly brighten their day.

A NOTE TO MY SON:

Dear Noah,

Once again, I'm suggesting that you try something out.

I'm going to send you a few blank note cards. You may also choose to recycle cards that you have received; just cut off the portion with the writing on it—folks usually leave the side opposite the note's cover blank. Or, next time you are in Target, swing by the card section and pick up a box of blank cards.

Set a goal of writing one card a week. Think of someone who makes you laugh or smile, or you are just glad that you know. Thank God for them. Jot down a few sentences to let them know that you are thinking about them and appreciate them. It doesn't need to be a letter or a big production. The whole thing should take you no more than five minutes.

Your note of appreciation will make their day. It will also make you more aware of others in your life. This awareness is, in itself, a practice of prayer.

Love you always,
Dad

A PRAYER FOR YOU:

Gracious God, make me mindful of others in the craziness of this busy day. Let me share words of appreciation with them as I lift up my gratitude to you for them. Bless my efforts so that others find affirmation in their daily living. Through Jesus Christ, amen.

CHAPTER SIX

LOOKING IN THE MIRROR

When you look upon yourself in a mirror, what do you see?

Was I to answer my question, I would have to say, "it depends." Is it first thing in the morning when I'm still groggy? Or is it at the end of the day when I'm exhausted? At neither of these times do I look pretty. I prefer the more presentable image after I've shaven, combed my receding hair, brushed my teeth, and dressed for the day. That is what I want others to see. It may not be Fabio, but it is as good as I'm going to look on any given day. You gotta go with what ya got.

Now, imagine if the mirror was magical and could reflect not only your exterior image but was also somehow able to reveal the interior. What would you see? Would you view genuine confidence or masked insecurity? Would you see a broken heart or an indomitable spirit? If through a magical mirror you could perceive your essence, would you be happy? Or would that visage bring you sorrow and despair?

In this final chapter of this devotional book, we will be looking in a mirror. Over the past five chapters, we have been considering transitions and life changes from the outside, inward. From thoughts about God (Holy Other) to creation, to fear/enemies, to the neighbor, we have been moving steadily closer to ourselves.

More than once, I've noted the counter-cultural nature of our progress. In a "me first" context, we automatically go to focusing on our needs, wants, and desires. Quickly turning inward, we miss the bigger picture and our proper place in relation to God, others, and creation. Whenever we mistakenly put ourselves in the center of the universe, where we don't belong, it is bound to get us into trouble.

At a time of transition or significant life change, the stakes are all that much higher. Obsessing about ourselves and what's within, we can miss the resources available to us in the networks and relationships of our lives. It is easy to overlook the blessings that God has gifted to us in the broader community.

That said, since we have taken the last chapters to explore this region beyond ourselves, it is about time that we look within. To ignore ourselves is folly. Back to the mirror.

When facing transitions in life, you may find it difficult to feel like and be the person you were before the changes. It might ring particularly true if the adjustment was severe, unexpected, traumatic, or unwelcome. On the other side of a sudden shift in life, we might find ourselves numb. No longer might you recognize the person that you see in the mirror (either the actual exterior or the magical interior.) Grief might cloud your vision or disfigure your reflection. Who is *that* in the mirror?

Returning to our core identity as a child of God can help. That is where we are heading during the final chapter of this book. We will work on developing our working theology to include the baptismal concept of being "beloved by God.'" The story that Jesus tells of two very different brothers and a father who loves extravagantly will assist in this effort. We'll take time to imagine what it means to be in the constant presence of God. The value of gratitude will allow us to appreciate life and the relationships we have in it in all circumstances. Driven by an ethic of generosity, we will find the courage to move beyond our fears of scarcity and share what we have and who we are with others. Finally, the last of our prayer practices involves breathing and centering.

Time to clean off our mirrors and find it within ourselves to look honestly at the person we see with all the love of God.

A NOTE TO MY SON:
Dear Noah,

This week I want to you think about yourself. Huh? What? Didn't I always tell you to think of others first? Yes—and you should. But I don't want you ever to forget that you are important and beloved in God's eyes, too. Don't overlook yourself.

You matter. A great deal, actually, and not just to your mother and me.

Not only did God create humanity in God's image, but God also created you. In you there lives the image of God.

As you care for others and this planet, be sure to take care of you. Take time to nurture your mind, body, and spirit. It's not selfish to do these things. It is essential if you want to make a difference beyond yourself.

Love you always,
Dad

A PRAYER FOR YOU:
Gracious God, when I look in the mirror, help me to see that I am your child. You have marked me with your love and grace. Help me to trust in your presence in each day, especially in those moments when I am most in need. Let me follow your lead into this day. Through Jesus Christ, amen.

Real Presence

Lutheran Christians have longed embraced the sacramental concept of "Real Presence." This idea, which dates back to Martin Luther himself, maintains that Christ is really present, *in, with, and under* the bread and the wine of communion. The bread and wine, within the context of eucharistic celebration, are the true body of

Christ given for our sake. When we commune, we physically take Jesus's life into our own.

The mechanics of this theological assertion has been one of debate between Lutherans and other Christians ever since Luther's time. For years, the discussion was divisive and kept Lutherans, Presbyterians, Methodists, and those of the other Reformed traditions apart and at odds. Thankfully, through ecumenical efforts over the last quarter-century, Full Communion agreements now exist between these Christian church bodies that allow for free and open celebration at Jesus's table. We have come to the point of being able to receive the gift of each other's sacramental perspective and recognize that what we have in common outweighs that which had separated us for centuries. These conversations hold the promise that someday all Christians (Protestants and Catholics alike) might once again share a common table.

Back to Real Presence. As a Lutheran pastor, who is grounded in weekly Word *and* Sacrament worship, I cling to God's promise to be fully present whenever we break the bread and share the cup. So real is God's presence that you can hold it in your hands, taste it in your mouth, and make it part of your body. When I stop and give it thought, it boggles my mind. Talk about a mystery! How can such things be?

A long time ago, when I was a seminary student, a supervising pastor, the Rev. Glenn Ludwig, shared his amazement with first communion students. Let me paraphrase. He told them that the more they received communion, the less they would understand…and the more they would be unable to live without it. Pastor Ludwig was right.

Part of what makes it hard to understand communion is life itself. Life is far messier than I imagined it to be in those first years of seminary. I've needed to navigate so many transitions and changes that I've lost count. Sure, there have been many unimaginable joys since then. But there have been sorrows as well.

Simplistic sacramental mechanics or formulas don't seem to hold up as well for me as a near-fifty-year-old as they did when I was in my early twenties. The certainty of ancient and unquestionable doctrines has faded behind the patina of experience. I find myself more and more open to mystery. I find I have less of a need to explain, understand, and define. I am more apt to lean into God's presence and content myself with *being*.

Leaning into God's presence is a sacramental act of receiving in faith. It is trusting that God will be faithful and present to us even if we don't have all the answers. When we break the bread, share the cup, pour the water, God shows up. What is more, God's presence is not a figment of our imagination, emotions, or cognitive construction. God is really there—as present as the hand of a friend that rests upon our shoulder or the comforting embrace of a loved one.

God desires communion and connection with our broken bodies. Luther talked about a "happy exchange:"

> Christ with all saints, by his love, takes upon himself our form, fights with us against sin, death, and all evil. This enkindles in us such love that we take on his form, rely upon this righteousness, life, and blessedness. And through the interchange of his blessings and our misfortunes, we become one loaf, one bread, one body, one drink, and have all things in common.[5]

---

[5] Martin Luther. *The Blessed Sacrament of the Holy and True Body of Christ, and the Brotherhoods* in Luther's Works Volume 35, (Philadelphia: Fortress Press, 1960), 58.

When we partake of the mysteries of communion, things get real. God links with us in such a way as to bring us life, strength, love, and ultimately hope. I find myself needing this life-generating and sustaining connection more and more. What a great God we have!

Although life remains complicated and changing, I have found respite, courage, and strength in the sure and certain hope of God's presence. Depending on the Sunday, I might drag, crawl, skip, run, bounce, or casually stroll to the communion table. Sometimes I'm filled with holy intention. At other times, I'm numb or distracted. No matter. Thankfully, God's presence doesn't depend upon my condition, ability, or construction. When into my hands is placed bread and cup, I know that God is present in a way that is oh-so-real.

A NOTE TO MY SON:

Dear Noah,

I am happy to hear that you have found your way to the Lutheran Campus Ministry worship. Weekly communion is such a gift. Although God is present in each breath that we take and in every moment of life, we forget such things. Sacraments help us to reconnect with the God who never leaves our side.

I'm glad you are attending worship, because as busy people, it is all too easy to skip this practice and disconnect from our faith. But faith is like the plant that we bought you for your dorm room. It takes your nurturing and care to thrive.

Faith is not a transaction. Going to worship and daily prayer are not coins that you can put into a sacred machine to make life perfect, successful, and rosy.

It is better to understand faith as a relationship that takes work and attention. Setting aside time to commune with God and others help. It won't make God love you more or be any closer. It will, instead, open your eyes and heart to recognize the awesome and very real presence of God that is as near as your next breath.

Love you always,
Dad

A PRAYER FOR YOU:

Gracious God, you come to us in the midst of our lives. Each moment holds the potential of sacramental encounter. Open our hearts to receive your presence. Strengthen our weary spirits with your strong love. Empower us to bear your life in such a way as to share your blessings with others so that they, too, might know your abiding presence. Through Jesus Christ, amen.

Letting Go of Our Inner Pharisee

"...Then the father said to him, "Son, you are always with me, and all that is mine is yours. But we had to celebrate and rejoice, because this brother of yours was dead and has come to life; he was lost and has been found.""

— Luke 15:31-32

Jesus told a group of his critics, who were having a hard time with his "open table" policy, a story about a family squabble that continues to be all too relatable.

Two very different brothers were vying for their father's love. The irresponsible one leaves home to squander a fortune. He pays no respect to his father and asks for his inheritance ahead of time. It is as though his father has become dead to him. The dependable son remains faithful, stays home, and shows the proper honor to his father.

All heck breaks loose: the wayward son returns home; the father welcomes him without restraint; the responsible son refuses to acknowledge his brother's existence. There is trouble in the family as feelings are hurt, verdicts levied, and hearts break.

It is a timeless tale that has a wide audience. Even non-Christians might be familiar with this Jesus story, which is traditionally labeled "the prodigal son." We might even hear someone refer to another, or themselves, as being the prodigal one in the family.

Often lost in the retelling of the story is the original audience and context. Jesus told this tale to those who were apt to judge. The Pharisees opposed Jesus's ministry, which reached out to the margins and shared God's hospitality with the outcast. According to the Pharisees, these people didn't deserve God's favor. Yet Jesus ate and shared table fellowship with those whom the Pharisees marked as "unclean" and not worthy of

God's attention. Like the older brother in the story, both their lack of compassion and grace consumed them.

This remains a tale that contains a pointed message, which speaks to the inner Pharisee within each of us. Somewhere in our spirit, there exists a cauldron where legalism and judgment combine to form a toxic poison that bubbles over. Whether we are prone to direct that venom on others or ourselves, it is invariably harmful and destructive. Relationships suffer from the strain of internal and external condemnation. Self-esteem withers under self-judgment.

The final episode of Jesus's story speaks directly to this detrimental phenomenon. In seething anger, the older brother refuses to enter the joy of his father. The forgiving father seeks him out and begs him to come to the feast, to be a part of the celebration. Forgiveness and reconciliation are the music that plays at the party to which the father has invited both his sons. Jesus leaves the story open-ended for us to complete.

How much authority and power will we give to our inner Pharisee? Will we allow this damaging influence to dominate our relationships with others? Will we let this voice shout within and make us feel unworthy to the core? Will we exclude ourselves from the party?

Or will we find the courage and wisdom to lean into God's grace? Forgiveness and reconciliation come to us as generous gifts from a God who refuses to let us go. It is a crazy idea—God loves us so much that no judgment in heaven, earth, or within can have the last word. God desires a life-giving connection with you and with me. Further, God wants us to extend that connection to others: family, friends, and strangers alike.

Through God's outpouring of love in Jesus, we find an invitation to join our voices in a jubilant song. Rejoice! Shout for joy! We have to sing, dance, and make merry.

Found are all the lost. Reunited are all the estranged. Included are all the discarded. Mercy has spoken louder than judgment. Love has silenced the Pharisee's objection as he or she enters the party.

A NOTE TO MY SON:

Dear Noah,

You know that "judgment" is a bad word at our house. You also know that we have all called each other on "judging." When we judge others with disapproving words, glances, or tones, we do damage. It is also true when we judge ourselves unworthy.

I'm not saying that we should abandon all critique. Seeking to better ourselves by measuring progress, effectiveness, and skill is not a bad thing. Improving ourselves and our work should be a lifelong aspiration.

That said, there is a difference between striving for excellence and beating up on ourselves or others for not being good enough. True worth comes not from what we do or produce or attain. Instead, it comes from being the person God made us be. Our value in life comes as a gift from God, and we express it best through loving and non-judging relationships with others.

Love you always,
Dad

A PRAYER FOR YOU:

Gracious God, your grace is more than I can imagine. Your mercy is grander than my faults. Your welcome alone can open the locked places of my heart. Be more to my less. Teach my stiff limbs to dance to the joyful music of Jesus's life. Through Jesus Christ, amen.

You Are Never Alone

Imagine you are all alone. There is no one around to help; no one in whom to confide, no one with whom to share the moment. Be it a storm, a medical emergency, or a plumbing crisis, the specific situation is subordinate to the fact that you are in trouble, scared, and by yourself. Adversity confronts you, and you must rise solo to face the challenge.

Though we have all been there a time or two, it is not a comfortable scenario. I'm not talking about the peace that solitude can bring for the introverted processors out there (I share your experience). There is nothing generative about being in a pinch and feeling like you are the only person in the world "to suffer the slings and arrows of outrageous fortune" and "take arms against a sea of troubles" (thanks, William!). Such an experience can give rise to utter despair.

It is also unnatural. In Genesis 2:18, we read, "Then the Lord GOD said, 'It is not good that the [human creature] should be alone; I will make him a helper as his partner.'" God created partnerships, family, and community so that we would never need to go it alone. God connects "me" to "we" for our mutual support and benefit.

Even though it runs counter to our dysfunctional national narrative of rugged individualism, God does not intend for us to fend for ourselves alone. Jesus chose twelve disciples—not one. None of them had bootstraps, either!

During life's significant changes and transitions, being alone is particularly hard. You wave to your family as they drive away after having moved your stuff into the dormitory. You close the front door of your home after having said goodbye to the last guest at the funeral. What do you do now? Quickly this question moves beyond the practical to the existential. What do *you*—all by yourself—*do* now? As it bounces within, a dreadful followup query accompanies that question: How am I going to make it alone?

It is here that sacred memory is of great support. We are *not* alone! God remains near. From the loneliness of exile, Isaiah's imagination reaches our spirit: "When you pass through the waters, I will be with you; and through the rivers, they shall not overwhelm you; when you walk through fire you shall not be burned, and the flame shall not consume you (Isaiah 43:2)." Even though Isaiah first spoke these words to an exiled nation during a time of unparalleled crisis, they ring true to individual hearts centuries later during a variety of personal calamities and challenges.

The waters of our baptism rise to fill our emptiness. No matter how trying the circumstances, God promises to always be with us. Even as you head back to your new dorm room or close that door on a house now missing a loved one, God remains. We belong to a loving God who will not let go.

Imagine that God is present, right beside you. In every moment, whether you sit in a crowd of friends and family or by yourself. In every place, whether you are in the familiar surroundings of your home or an unknown space. You are never truly alone.

Breathe and lean into God's presence. Find peace where words lose all their power to describe and control. *Be.* Feel the assurance of love that passes all understanding. Enter the space that the saints of old occupied in their struggles and tribulations. Rest in faith and discover respite for your weary body. Close your eyes, put up your feet, and allow a fresh breath of air to fill your innermost parts. Stay as long as it takes to experience the truth that your faith believes with every fiber of your being: you are not alone; God is near.

From that connected place, find your way to communion with others. What new friendships await your discovery? Where will you experience God's presence in the face and kindness of those in your life? How will those who are both familiar and unknown present the face of Christ to you? How might you shine Christ's love to them?

Imagine that it is time to leave the dark solitude of your tomb and live in the daylight of resurrected community.

A NOTE TO MY SON:

Dear Noah,

It must have been hard for you on moving day when we drove away. It was the strangest feeling for me. I know that we couldn't stay for as long as I wanted to—heck, if that were the case, I'd still be there!

I remember the first time I was dropped off by my parents at seminary. I watched their SUV (they had one way before it was a popular vehicle) drive over the hill and felt like I was all alone. And I was. I didn't know anybody there. The familiar faces of those who loved me were driving away. I was by myself and needed to blaze a new trail into uncharted territory.

You might still be blazing your trail, trying to find your way through unknown crowds of people. Give it time. Breathe. Remember, connections don't happen overnight. Put yourself in places where you have a chance of making friendships.

And remember: you are never alone. Not only do you have your family's love with you, but you also have God's. This is the same God, who through the waters of your baptism, claimed your life and declared it to be beloved. God is with you and goes with you into your future. Lean into this truth, and may you find in it rest for your weary soul and companionship for your journey.

Love you always,
Dad

A PRAYER FOR YOU:
Gracious God, you remain near even when I feel all alone. Make me aware of your presence on the darkest and loneliest of days. Let me find in you the connection that I need to remain engaged in life. Resurrect me from the despair of each tomb so that I might live in the hope of each new day. Through Jesus Christ, amen.

Gratitude

Back in college, I attended a summer clown camp held on the campus of the University of Wisconsin, LaCrosse. It was for adults who were amateur or semi-professional clowns. The instructors came from all over the children's entertainment business, and some even had Ringling Brothers, Barnum and Bailey Circus acclaim. I learned a lot about clowning as an art form—something I needed, as I had just started clowning at parades, Sunday schools, and the local hospital. With a few others, including my brother John, I formed a clown troupe at my home church. We were busy, traveling all around northeastern New Jersey.

Before long, my brother and I started to get requests to do birthday parties. The children we encountered seemed to like us, so the parents wanted to book us at their next event. Suddenly, John and I were "clowns for hire." We must have done a dozen parties or so. Word was traveling, and we developed a good reputation. Plus, we were cheap! All the ingredients for "overnight" success. Except we didn't go in that direction.

There was something markedly different between our clowning venues. Whenever we visited patients in the hospital, handing out paper roses made by my grandpa, or performed for children in the inner city, there was a sense of gratitude. In contrast, whenever we did a birthday party for children in the suburbs, that feeling was missing. Sure, we got paid for the party, but our work wasn't appreciated. The kids at the parties expected entertainment; often, their little unappreciative selves were downright rude.

Don't get me wrong, the money was nice. In the end, however, we went for the smiles and thanks. We followed our hearts, not our wallets. We shifted our clowning efforts to where they made the most impact. The experiences which followed were rich and transformational. That's what helped me decide to go to seminary and become a Lutheran pastor.

In my two decades of serving as a pastor in suburban contexts, I have noticed that, at times, there can be a lack of gratitude and appreciation. Perhaps it is because folks are incredibly busy—too busy to stop, breathe, and smell the roses, never mind give thanks for them. Or maybe certain things become expected when you have more disposable income. We demand that lines be short in the grocery store and that people go out of their way to serve our needs and whims.

The value of gratitude can be in short supply in a culture where folks consume, acquire, and spend at rapid rates. I'm not sure we even recognize what is happening; our consumptive behavior has consumed us! We don't realize the need for gratitude. And community, relationships, and our personal selves suffer as a result.

Eucharist was a critical value in early Christian communities. In ancient Greek, *eucharist* means thanksgiving. Sacrament-minded Christian communities use this word to describe the ritual meal also known as Holy Communion. Not only did the first followers of Jesus break bread and share in regular eucharistic celebration, but the New Testament elevates the value of thanksgiving within the community. Eucharist was more than a meal; it was a communal value.

The apostle Paul speaks regularly of giving thanks for the Christians in the various cities to which he writes. For example, Paul addressed those who live in Philippi, saying: "I thank my God every time I remember you, constantly praying with joy in every one of my prayers for all of you, because of your sharing in the Gospel from the first day until now (Philippians 1:3-5)." Sharing thanks is a sacred endeavor and not to be overlooked.

When Paul takes the time to be grateful, he recognizes the relationship and connection that he shares with others. What is more, appreciative of the kindness and presence of others, Paul experiences gratitude to God. Since God is the source of all good things, when we express thanks to others, we are also thanking God.

Stepping off the treadmill of suburban insanity to give thanks is a good thing for us to do for our spirit. Following in Paul's footsteps, we become aware of the many connections in life, wherein we can experience God's blessings. We step away from the lie that we are at the center of the universe long enough to realize a larger truth. God has linked our lives with the lives of others and the whole of creation.

We are networked and interdependent by God's design. Because of others, we are. Our joys and sorrows, laughter and tears, are related to others. Giving thanks for the presence and work of others acknowledges our need for them and their need for us.

Thinking back, that was what was happening all those years ago when I wore greasepaint and donned a bright red wig. When I set foot in the hospital room of a sick child, I entered the space of their need for laughter. God blessed my silly antics, resulting in their smiles and joy. In a child's expression of gratitude, I received a blessing. In turn, I was grateful for their response. Gratitude—eucharist—is a cyclical value that returns blessings upon blessing. In all of it, God is wonderfully present.

A NOTE TO MY SON:

Dear Noah,

How many times have you said "thank you" to someone today? If you can recall the exact number, you need to put "express gratitude" at the top of your to-do list for tomorrow. Giving thanks ought to be a continuous action, so automatic that you couldn't possibly count how often you do it.

When you appreciate someone or something else, you are stopping to recognize the gift that others are in your life. That gift comes from God and emanates through their kindness, generosity, and actions. Thanking them and thanking God is much more than a nice (or even right) thing to do. It means choosing to live a life that acknowledges the critical connections we have with others.

Centering yourself in the value of gratitude, you will discover a richness, depth, and blessedness to life that you would otherwise pass over.

Love you always,
Dad

A PRAYER FOR YOU:

Gracious God, all the blessings of life come from you. Thank you for the many ways that your love and grace come to me through the lives of others and your good creation. Give me the wisdom to stop multiple times along today's journey to acknowledge and appreciate your gifts. Let "thank you" flow generously and regularly from my lips. Through Jesus Christ, amen.

Generosity

I distinctly remember the night, even though it was almost twenty-five years ago. It was at the end of my pastoral internship in Utica, New York. A bunch of Lutheran pastors took their significant others out to dinner at a Mexican restaurant in a nearby town. It was a pretty nice place, and the food was excellent. At the end of the meal, each couple received their bill in a small folder. When I opened mine, I found out that one of the other pastors had picked up the tab for the intern and his future wife. What a nice surprise! To this day, I continue to appreciate that kind gift.

Have you ever found yourself the recipient of someone else's generosity? Ever have a stranger pay for your coffee? Or perhaps someone was abundant in sharing their time and patience with you.

When someone is generous, they go above and beyond expectations. Because generosity departs from the usual way things go, it can create wonder and sincere appreciation. It has the potential to build and strengthen relationships between giver and receiver. It inspires additional acts of generosity.

Generosity as a spiritual ethic begins with the recognition that all we have in life comes from God. Our selves, our time, and our possessions all have the potential to connect us with God's gracious abundance. Sharing what we have and who we are with others is a response to God's activity in our life, making generosity a sacred endeavor.

If our act of giving to others expects nothing in return, then it is an offering. When we give, we offer something to the happiness, sustenance, or advancement of another. Rest assured: when we express such care, God smiles. Our actions can provide a practical example of loving one's neighbor in real time.

No matter the size of your investment portfolio (or even if you have one), all people can be generous. It is not so much a function of wealth as it is of vision. Do you see life through the freeing lens of abundance or do you see it as limited and scarce? Are you willing to take a risk in giving away something that you might need yourself?

Some of the most significant generosity that I've witnessed has involved great courage on the part of folks who didn't have a lot of material wealth. They gave because another was in need, not because they had a lot of extras lying around. Again, it is a vision thing. When you see life as a gift and all that you have as a gift from God, it is easier to give.

A miser's heart, on the other hand, is convinced that life is a losing battle in which we are all a few steps away from desolation. Hold onto what you have. A rainy day is coming for sure. You fear having nothing after giving everything away.

Generosity is a choice. We choose to see through the lens of abundance or not. We decide to take the risk of giving away things we might use in the future. We determine to live in the abundant blessings of God and not by the anxious scarcity of the world. Or we don't.

What have I to give? What if you don't feel all that rich right now? Perhaps you are waiting for some time in the future when you will be more flush with resources?

Again, from observing the habits of generous people, this ethic is best not postponed for the "perfect" time. Either folk practice generosity or they don't. You either live courageously, trusting that there is enough, that you have and will have enough, or you live with sheepish restraint. It is a matter of perception and prioritizing. It is about seeing others less as a threat and competition and more as siblings and an opportunity to give.

After years of working in parishes with a great disparity of resources, a pastor of mine once shared the wisdom of his experience: you will not find an unhappy giver, and you will never see a happy miser. Ultimately, generous people tap into life's joy in a way that those who don't give will never experience.

Generous people reflect the generosity of God, which brings people together, heals the sick, accompanies the lonely, forgives the hardened sinner, and raises the dead.

Further, generosity is generative; it begets life that is rich beyond compare.

Who doesn't want to live that life?

A NOTE TO MY SON:
Dear Noah,

I'll ask the question right out: Are you generous? Do you share what you have with others?
Don't wait until you make your millions, acquire all manner of wealth and fortune, or have extra time to spare before you choose to be generous. First of all, there is a lot of living to happen before any of that happens (if it ever does). Second, generosity takes practice and is more a way of living abundantly than anything else. Generosity comes from your heart and not from the storehouse of your surplus.

Find the joy in giving to others. Experience the true riches of this lifestyle before material wealth and riches get in your way. Don't wait to learn generosity—there will never be a perfect time in the future but for the present.

Love you always,
Dad

A PRAYER FOR YOU:

Gracious God, you are generous beyond measure. You have so richly blessed all creation with your goodness. Give me the wisdom to see that your abundance surrounds me. Teach me to give generously. Let me share in the joy that comes from sharing your blessings. Through Jesus Christ, amen.

Breathe

I used to think that prayer was "talking with God." Depending on the situation, this conversation ranged from a casual chat with a friend to formal plea before a powerful authority figure. I was concerned about using the correct words. Was I using the right words, both in addressing God and in raising my prayer? Was my language holy and proper enough? What were my motivations? Were they pure enough? Sincere enough?

Have you ever fretted about prayer and what to say to God?

Although I reminded myself to relax, be my genuine self, and talk to God as a friend, I found that my words were less than satisfactory. It seemed like I was always trying to work some deal. Even when I was offering a prayer of thanks and praise, I found myself trying to get on God's good side. A little extra praise never hurts; right?

I was using words in a transactional fashion to manipulate the Divine. My words disassembled the conversation into a one-sided monologue. I'm not sure I did this maliciously, or even intentionally. But my endless chatter was not very prayerful or humble. Like a child who demands candy in a supermarket, prayer was all about me seeking to get my way.

It took many years and the insight of many wise people (like my spiritual director—thanks, Dick!) to bring me to a more relational and incarnational understanding and practice of prayer. I now envision prayer more as leaning into the presence of God with my whole being. When I pray, I seek to enter a space of connection where conversations become silenced.

Taking deep breaths allows my whole body to participate. Prayer moves from something that I construct in my head and heart to something that I experience right down to my gut. As I breathe, instead of forcing my words, ideas, needs, concerns, manipulations, deals, and demands upon God, I push the words away. Prayer is not about me getting God's attention so as to get God to act as I wish but about me receiving God's presence, which is already near. Casting words aside, I seek to be in the space where I might listen and be the beloved child that God created in the first place.

Silent prayer centered in breathing has been transformative for me. I have found in the sacredness of silence a place that engages my being like nothing else can. Gone are the worries about getting the words of my prayer right so I might impress God and "get candy," so to speak. In place of my previous concern is a desire to rest and find renewal in God's being, which is as close as my next full and unhurried breath.

This is not to say that I no longer use words in prayer. I do. I still find it necessary to express myself to God using my words. That's especially true when I'm praying on behalf of another or for some concern that weighs heavy on my heart. But I no longer rely on words exclusively, nor even primarily when I pray.

Let me briefly walk you through my prayer practice.

Find a comfortable place to sit or kneel. If kneeling, you might want to make or find yourself a kneeling bench. For starters, I'd suggest that you locate a quiet place. After some practice, you might be able to pray in this way in a busy place; I have used silent, breathing prayer in airports and train stations.

Set your phone, watch, or a kitchen timer for the amount of time that you have to pray. I suggest taking at least five or seven minutes. You might need to work up to this length. Setting a timer takes time out of the equation. This way, you don't need to worry about running late on a busy day.

Close your eyes. Take a deep breath. Let the air fill your whole body. Welcome the air as Spirit (in the language of the New Testament, air and spirit share the same word: *pneuma*). Receive the gift of Spirit deep within yourself. Exchange the contents of your lungs with the fresh breath of God that surrounds your body. In and out.

Clear your mind of any thoughts, schedules, words. Rest in nothing but the presence of God. You are beloved by your creator. Warts and all. Imperfections and vulnerabilities. God entered time and space for your sake. Let the body of Christ come into your body with each breath you take. Let God fill your being.

Delight in God's presence like a child bouncing a balloon on a warm, sunny day. For a moment, let your cares drift away. Let nothing get in your way during your time with God. Stay in this moment for as long as you can.

Don't worry about the time. Remember, you set the timer. Breathe deeply throughout. Keep pushing those stray thoughts away. When your time is up, take one final breath. Let this breath fill you with gratitude. Thank God for the peace, calm, and renewed sense of God's presence.

It is my prayer (I know—I'm using words again) that this prayer practice might be as much a gift for you as it has become for me. May you find peace and rest for your weary soul during your time of transition.

A NOTE TO MY SON:

Dear Noah,

Did you take a moment to breathe today? I know that our bodies do this automatically, or at least, that's what is needed for us to survive. But have you stopped long enough in your busy day to be aware of your breath?

Close your eyes. Quickly. Inhale the biggest breath that you can take. Let it expand your lungs and your whole body. Let it out. If no one is around, allow your exhale to sound out like you do when you blow into your trumpet.

Know that no matter what this day might bring, God is with you and in you. Let God's love for you fill your whole being. Delight in it. Smile at it. Be grateful. And don't forget to share it.

Love you always,
Dad

A PRAYER FOR YOU:

Gracious God, you are the breath of all life. Your presence animates all living things. Make me aware of your presence in me so that I might honor, delight, and center my actions in your love. Guide me in my breathing so that I might direct my living toward you. Through Jesus Christ, amen.

CHAPTER SEVEN

CONCLUSION

When I started writing this book, I was keen on sharing insights about the life of faith that I've gleaned from more than two decades of being a Lutheran pastor. I wanted to provide my son, Noah, with encouraging and useful words as he began university. From experience, I know that life can be hard and confusing, particularly during times of transition. I also know that our faith can be a tremendous resource when navigating unknown circumstances. From the place of parental love, I sought to shine a little light to make his way a touch brighter.

In the process of writing, I discovered something about myself: when it comes to matters of faith, I am still on a journey. My life and theology are still in the process of becoming. I continue to wonder, learn, grow, live, and even die in my faith.

Even as I seek to nurture others (like my sons and those in the congregation which I serve) in spiritual matters, my faith needs constant nurturing as well. Oh, sure, we are all in different places in our faith development. But it would be spiritually arrogant to think I have "arrived" and have all the answers in all matters of faith. I don't. What is more, even if I live a hundred years more, I still won't. The life of faith is one of constant "becoming."

Throughout this book, I expressed the need to hone a working theology. Whether we want to admit it or not, we are all theologians insofar as we all have ideas about God. Even the staunch atheist is a theologian; he or she thinks God doesn't exist. Consciously examining, refining, and reshaping our "God-ideas" is an essential task that helps keep our relationship with God in the front of our minds. Again, I share this wisdom from the place of one who works daily on my thoughts about God.

Even though I have multiple theological degrees from accredited institutions of higher learning hanging on the wall of my church study, faith requires that I regularly test my assumptions about God. I have to hold up my God-ideas against the background of my experience to see if they are still valid. Most of the time, I find that it only takes a minor tweaking to make things fit. That said, there have been occasions that have rocked my world, necessitating major renovations to my working theology.

When this happens, I scramble to pull in as many resources as I can. I seek the wisdom of trusted teachers and mentors. I revisit at the foundational teachings of my faith tradition and might even crack open my Book of Concord (this contains foundational documents for Lutheran churches such as Martin Luther's Small and Large Catechisms). I'll pray to ask God for guidance and to keep me open during the time of discernment. And I'll turn to the stories of Jesus in the Gospels.

Another realization that I came to in writing this book is how important the stories of Jesus are to me. They inform not only my working theology but also my values and ethics. I am both comforted and challenged by these familiar stories, which spark my spiritual imagination and cause me to wonder.

As I read them, they invite me to lean into God's grace even as they push back boundaries and question my previous assumptions. For example, Jesus's radical table fellowship makes me question my judgment and exclusion of others. Because of Jesus's insistence on eating with outcasts, sinners, and tax collectors, inclusivity is a Gospel orientation. As a follower of Jesus, I am invited to go and do likewise.

Sometimes I will find the courage to step beyond my comfort zone. When that happens, I often discover new joy. Other times, my lack of love shames me. It is at those moments that I realize that the Jesus stories of forgiveness and mercy are for me. Joy returns as Jesus, once again, invites even the likes of me to the table.

In addition to appreciating the stories of Jesus anew, I have realized how critical prayer is to my life. Now, this may seem strange to you. You might even snicker and say, "Of course prayer is essential to you. After all, you *are* a pastor—a professional purveyor of prayers for all occasions!" Truck drivers drive eighteen-wheelers; pilots fly planes; teachers educate classrooms filled with students; and pastors pray. Thank you, Captain Obvious, for appearing and revealing all sorts of unnecessary observations!

Chuckles aside, it is one thing to say prayers in a professional capacity and it is still another to locate prayer at the core of one's walk with God. Throughout all my seminary training, I was not required to take a class on personal prayer or demonstrate that prayer was part of my spiritual growth. There might have been a few opportunities along the way to learn about prayer, but there wasn't a concerted effort (on either my part or the seminary's) to develop prayer practices as a foundation for ministry.

It wasn't until I was in the parish and well-versed in praying for others that I came to a place where I needed to work on personal prayer practices. There was a bit of shame involved. It felt a little hypocritical to pray so much for others and not so much for myself.

Through my years of being a pastor, a hunger for a closer walk with God has emerged in my being. I am grateful for the opportunity to take a sabbatical in my eighteenth year of ordained ministry, during which I was able to explore spirituality apart from the professional demands of being a pastor. Guided by the wisdom of my spiritual director, the Rev. Dick Bruesehoff, I was able to connect on a deeper level with God. Prayer was inseparable from this effort.

What is more, I discovered that silent prayer was the practice that most nurtured my spirit. When I focused on breathing and pushing all other thoughts from my mind, a sacred space emerged for me. In that space, I was able to delight as a child of God in a new way. As I tended my prayer life, I found a new strength for not only my public ministry but also my personal life.

Prayer has become, for me, an essential communicative link with my Creator. When I take the time to pray, I make a space of openness within my being. I welcome the Divine dance partner and embrace with all the intensity of a lover. Through being attentive to spiritual matters, I have found a more fulfilling path to travel.

Whether praying, reflecting on the stories of Jesus to light my imagination and inform my values and ethics, or developing my working theology, the common theme here is that of intentionality. For faith to be a valuable resource in navigating life's turbulent and changing waters, it requires some effort on our part.

Faith is not a can of soda that sits on the shelf until we are thirsty. Sure, you can approach it like that, but don't be surprised if you find things a little flat when you open it up. Faith is organic and living; it is a relationship and certainly not a product.

I have seen the sad scenario time and again. People who never took the time to nurture and grow their faith find themselves in a quandary when the proverbial excrement hits the fan. They jump into prayer with unrealistic expectations that everything will suddenly turn out. When it does (hey, miracles *do* happen sometimes), they quickly forget God and fall back into old patterns of inattention. When the situation doesn't resolve according to their liking, which is the more realistic scenario, they are angry at God. They conclude that faith is fake.

Folks, it doesn't work like that! Don't blame God, whom you have not engaged, for being absent when you are in dire need. God remains, but your (and my) "untrained" heart has difficulty perceiving this reality.

For faith to be a force of vitality, comfort, and assistance in life, you need to be intentional about nurturing it on a regular (I'll even say *daily*) basis. Put simply, faith takes work. Our faith requires our intentional efforts.

What is this? Is Walt a closet Pelagian? (In the fifth century, the church declared Pelagius a heretic on account of his teaching that humans can earn their salvation through good works.) Didn't Martin Luther rail against works?

No, I am still a theologian of grace. I maintain the belief that is at the heart of my Lutheran upbringing, training, and preaching: faith comes as a gift from a loving God. There is nothing that we can do to make God love us any more—or any less. God loves us unconditionally. Salvation comes to us through God's action, mercy, and steadfast love. Period.

Our response to that love and grace, though not necessary for salvation, is essential to life. We can decide to follow in the path of Jesus's outward-directed love or indulge ourselves in self-adoration. Either way, God's love will remain the same. Again, God's graceful love is not dependent upon our action.

Does that mean that we can live a self-centered, greedy, obnoxious existence, disregarding the needs, feelings, and presence of others? Aren't we supposed to show compassion, kindness, and patience in our dealings with others? Doesn't God want us to live as Jesus did?

We have the freedom to decide how we are going to relate to others, to the world around us, and to God. We can be kind, or we can be a stinker. It is our choice. There are consequences to both paths. In the course of our living, we will either endear ourselves to others or be repulsive to them. The adage about making the bed you lie in applies here. Our relationships are both strengthen and weakened by our actions.

Since God desires for all creation to live in harmony and *shalom* (peace/wholeness), pathways that move in the direction of building up, nurturing, care, community, inclusion, and hospitality are preferred. In short, when we make loving choices, we participate in helping to bring about God's desired outcome for life. To use New Testament imagery, we are taking part in bringing God's Kingdom into being. When we do, God smiles. There is joy in heaven and on earth.

It is also true that God will not stop loving. Based on the life of Jesus, love is the way that God chooses to relate to creation. No matter how poorly we live, God will love. Divine love is unconditional and does not depend upon us getting it "right." Grace is grace. Period.

Back to intentionality. When I was a teenager, I received a gift of a remote control foam glider from my parents. It came in a large cardboard box and required some assembly. On Christmas morning, when I unwrapped the box, I took out all the pieces and carefully laid them out. To build something that would soar in the sky was a cool idea that ignited my imagination. I couldn't wait. Then I put the many parts back into the box. And that is where they stayed: in a box in the corner of my childhood room. Although I owned a plane, I never put it together, and it never took flight. My dreams for the plane-in-a-box remained unrealized.

Faith needs some assembly. Though it comes to us as a gift from a loving God, if we let it stay in the box, hidden in the corner, we will never experience the joy of flight. Bit by bit, part by part, we assemble our spiritual selves. Over time, with the help of others, influenced by experiences, we move in the direction of the heavens. We yearn to be able to soar with God.

Another way to think about living faith is to use the metaphor of dance. God invites us onto the dance floor and begins to lead in the direction of love. Music and movement swirl around us. We lean into the joy-filled nature of it all. Soon, we find ourselves propelled around the room. From time to time, we might stumble or miss a step, especially when the music changes tempo and style. Trusting in our partner, however, we adjust our dance and find a new flow. There is a joy as we dance the night away.

In conclusion, I am grateful for the journey of faith which I find myself walking. Through ups and downs, advances and setbacks, unknowns and discoveries, the travel is rarely dull. I am grateful for my fellow companions on the way—my life partner Katie, family, friends, mentors, colleagues, church—for their wisdom, strength, encouragement, sustenance, and love. I am also appreciative of my two sons, Noah and Mark, and for the opportunity to be their father. They inspire me on a daily basis and have allowed me to grow as a person and in my faith. They have shared love with me and lighted my way. With thanks, I go and grow with love.

ABOUT THE AUTHOR

Ordained in 1997 as a pastor in the Evangelical Lutheran Church in America, The Rev. Dr. Walt Lichtenberger has served two congregations: Faith Lutheran Church in New Providence, New Jersey and St. James Lutheran Church in Burnsville, Minnesota.

In addition to over two decades of parish experience, he holds three advanced theological degrees. In 1997, he graduated from the Lutheran Theological Seminary in Gettysburg with a Masters of Divinity. This was followed in 2006, with a Masters of Sacred Theology from the Lutheran Theological Seminary in Philadelphia. In 2012, Walt graduated from Union Presbyterian Seminary in Richmond, Virginia with a Doctor of Ministry.

Walt lives with his wife and two sons in Savage, Minnesota.

Walt maintains a website filled with devotional materials that he has written. *Light From This Hill* is dedicated to shining a little light on your path. If you are interested in finding out more visit: www.lightfromthishill.com.

Made in the USA
Columbia, SC
17 March 2019